THE LEOPARD'S SPOTS

THE LEOPARD'S SPOTS
Biblical and African Wisdom
in Proverbs

Friedemann W. Golka

T&T CLARK
EDINBURGH

T&T CLARK LTD
59 GEORGE STREET
EDINBURGH EH2 2LQ
SCOTLAND

First Published 1993

ISBN 0 567 09636 X

Typeset by Type Aligne, Edinburgh
Printed and bound in Great Britain by Bookcraft, Avon

To Claus Westermann,

the Heidelberg Old Testament scholar

and my teacher,

and to the memory of his father,

Diedrich Westermann,

the late Berlin Africanist.

Contents

Preface

This book has a history of 25 years, and neither I nor my friends believed it would ever get written. When I began my doctoral research on *the Aetiologies in the Old Testament*, it was my supervisor, Claus Westermann, in Heidelberg who first directed my interest towards folklore and social anthropology. During my time at Oxford (1968-70) I attended occasional lectures at the Institute of Social Anthropology and, a few years later, while lecturing in Old Testament at the University of Exeter, was able to come back to consult the late Professor Sir Edward Evans-Pritchard on extra-biblical flood stories in connection with my doctoral research.

After completing my doctorate, my interest turned to the biblical proverbs. Even my brief contact with Social anthropology made me realize that biblical proverbs were very similar to African ones. Hence I took them to be indigenous folk proverbs and felt that Old Testament scholarship was barking up the wrong tree when claiming that they were literary works of art, much influenced by the civilizations of Egypt and Mesopotamia. Claus Westermann confirmed my suspicion in his article, "Weisheit im Sprichwort", *Forschung am Alten Testament 2*, Munich 1974, pp.149-61. He, too, was using African proverbial material which he had inherited from his own father, Diedrich Westermann, the late Berlin Africanist (Jakob Spieth, Die *Ewe-Stämme*, 1906, pp.599-612).

By then Norman Whybray had already annihilated the hypothesis of a 'professional class of wise men' (R.N. Whybray, *The Intellectual Tradition in the Old Testament*, BZAW 135, Berlin 1974). So, I opened up my attack on the other two main fronts with two articles in *Vetus Testamentum* on the 'school' hypothesis ("Die israelitische Weisheitsschule oder 'Des Kaisers neue Kleider'", *VT* 33, 1983, pp.257-70) and on the 'royal court' hypothesis ("Die Königs- und Hofsprüche und der Ursprung der israelitischen Weisheit", *VT* 36, 1986, pp.13-36). These now form the first two chapters of this book. Further support came from a pupil of Roland Murphy's, Carole R. Fontaine, *Traditional Sayings in the Old Testament*, Sheffield 1982. Her investigations of proverb performance also pointed to popular origin.

1

The 1980s then saw an interruption of my work on Proverbs. George Knight asked me to write 'Jonah' for the International Theological Commentary, on which I spent my study leave from the University of Exeter in 1985 and which appeared in 1988. It was the need to contribute to the Festschrift for Claus Westermann's 80th birthday in 1989 which brought me back to the proverbial fold. "Die Flecken des Leoparden. Biblische und afrikanische Weisheit im Sprichwort" (in: *Schöpfung und Befreiung*, FS C. Westermann, ed.s R. Albertz, F.W. Golka, J. Kegler, Stuttgart 1989, pp.149-65) now forms ch.3 of this book and has given it its title.

In 1990 the Society for the Study of Theology asked me to write a paper, entitled "Creation and Wisdom", for their conference at St Andrews. This forced me to consider the theological implications of my work on Hebrew wisdom - a very necessary exercise for an Old Testament scholar. This paper appears now as ch.7 of this book. Dr Geoffrey Green, the Managing Director of T & T Clark, was present at the SST conference, and in conversation with him the idea for the present book was born. He guided its completion with patience and care.

During the summer semester 1992 the University of Oldenburg granted me study leave, after only having appointed me to the chair of Old Testament in October 1989. I was able to spend it in Oxford where the central chapters on 'Rich and Poor'; 'Law, Crime, and Justice'; and 'Family and Kinship' have been written. I should like to thank the Principal, staff, and students of Wycliffe Hall for their hospitality, and Professor John Davis, Chairman of the Oxford University Institute of Social and Cultural Anthropology, Dr Wendy James, and the Librarian, Mike Morris, for their help and advice.

As an appendix to this book I have included a paper on 'The Biblical Joseph Story and Thomas Mann's Novel', which was first given in Oldenburg as a public lecture in 1990, then at the International Meeting of the Society of Biblical Literature in Rome in 1991, and to colleagues at Oxford and Birmingham in 1992. I thank all these colleagues for their helpful comments. As Gerhard von Rad has frequently emphasized the Wisdom background of the Joseph story, this appendix is not unrelated to the topic of my book.

My friends, Alastair Logan, Peter Sedgwick, Dan Cohn-Sherbok, Rodney Annis, and Stephen Laird, have kindly given of their time to help with proof reading. English proof readers are extremely hard to come by in Oldenburg.

Most of all I have to thank my Heidelberg teacher, Claus Westermann, for his patient encouragement over these many years. In his retirement he has now published his own account of early Hebrew wisdom, *Wurzeln der Weisheit. Die ältesten Sprüche Israels und anderer Völker*, Göttingen 1990. This will make my debt to him even more apparent.

Oldenburg, September 1992

Friedemann W. Golka

1

The Israelite Wisdom School or 'The Emperor's New Clothes'

Rolf Rendtorff's work on the Pentateuch[1] which appeared in 1977 is important not so much because of the solution which he proposes, but because of the incontrovertible evidence that the 'consensus of scholarship' during the last 30 years had been built on very shaky foundations. So far scholars had tried to combine the assumption of continuous sources with the form-critical and traditio-historical method of starting from the 'smallest units'. Now scholars were shocked by Rendtorff's claim "that both methods...in their starting-point are diametrically opposed to each other" (p.1).

After this wholesome shock we may ask ourselves whether there are other areas in Old Testament research where certain and verifiable results have been replaced by the 'consensus of scholarship'. In my opinion this has foremost been the case in the field of Wisdom. Before the 'Wisdom fashion' caused by the works of von Rad considerably fewer scholars have done any independent research in this area, compared to the Pentateuch, the Historical books, the Prophets or the Psalms. Furthermore, von Rad's position in Wisdom research was so outstanding that the adoption of a hypothesis by him was equal to a process of 'canonisation' and seemed to remove the need to question this hypothesis any further.

A clear example of a hypothesis maintained only by the 'consensus of scholarship' is the claimed existence of schools in Israel during the early monarchy. There is no biblical evidence for these institutions. The first mention of a school occurs in the 2nd century B.C. (Sir. 51.23) – 800 years after David and Solomon! It was an equally hypothetical 'class of wise men'

---

(1) *Das überlieferungsgeschichtliche Problem des Pentateuch*, BZAW 147 (Berlin and New York, 1977)

4

that is supposed to have taught in these schools. To them scholars attribute (a) the collection of popular wisdom, or (b) the creation of literary wisdom, or (c) a combination of both.

It follows that, in searching for the origin of Israelite Wisdom, we shall have to solve the question of the existence of schools. In tracing the ancestry of the school hypothesis one eventually comes upon August Klostermann.[2] I find it difficult to imagine that many Old Testament scholars alive today have actually read Klostermann's work which appeared in the Zahn-Festschrift in 1908. Its title is quoted very frequently, as one now apparently 'knows' since then that there were schools in ancient Israel. We shall, therefore, have to begin with an examination of Klostermann's arguments.

Klostermann was the first to realize that the existence of schools in Israel would have to be proved from the Old Testament itself. He was no longer satisfied with the Egyptian and Mesopotamian analogies. Unfortunately, he was not very successful in his enterprise. He was only able to provide a mere three texts which allegedly presupposed the working of a school: Isa. 50.4-9; Isa. 28.9-13, and Prov. 22.17-21.

Before we examine these texts in detail, let us consider Klostermann's method. A child of his time, he takes refuge to conjecture and emendations to such an extent that in some cases the text is hardly recognizable. I, therefore, dare to claim that none of the scholars who are basing their arguments on Klostermann could possibly approve of his methods after closer examination. His results, however, are being continuously repeated by the very same scholars.

Klostermann's third example, Prov. 22.17-21, is quickly dealt with. When publishing his essay, he was simply ignorant of the fact that Prov. 22.17-21 is closely based on the Egyptian Wisdom book *Amen-em-ope*. The papyrus in question had already been bought by the British Museum in 1888, but it was not published until 1923.[3] Only the two following years saw the guiding publications by A. Erman and H. Gressmann, who pointed to the significance of *Amen-em-ope* for Prov. 22.17 - 23.11.[4]

Klostermann's observation that Prov. 22.17-21 represents "a teacher's

(2)   "Schulwesen im alten Israel", *FS Theodor Zahn* (Leipzig, 1908), pp. 193-232.

(3)   E.A. Wallis, *Facsimiles of Hieratic Papyri in the British Museum*, Second Series (London, 1923), Tab. I-XIV, and pp. 9-18, 41-51.

(4)   A. Erman, "Das Weisheitsbuch des Amen-em-ope", *OLZ 27* (1924), col. 241-52; idem, "Eine ägyptische Quelle der Sprüche Salomos", *SAB* (1926), pp. 86-93, Tab. VI-VII; H. Gressmann, "Die neugefundene Lehre des Amen-em-ope und die vorexilische Spruchdichtung Israels", *ZAW 42* (1924), pp. 272-96; idem, *Israels Spruchweisheit im Zusammenhang der Weltliteratur* (Berlin, 1925).

farewell discourse to his pupil" (p. 231) is, therefore, quite correct. But he is not entitled to claim "that in the old Israelite schools the teacher dictated what the pupil had to write and that the pupil was expected to reproduce these dictations from memory" (ibid). Prov. 22.17-21 has to be explained against the background of the Egyptian instructions. For pre-exilic Israel this text represents no evidence at all. And this in turn cuts Klostermann's proof texts to those humble two from the Book of Isaiah.

Let us begin with Isa. 28.9-13, with vv. 9 and 10 being the important ones. Presumably at a sacrifice in the Jerusalem temple[5] Isaiah spies out the drunken priests and cultic prophets and reprimands them. They, however, the professionals, do not take very kindly to being reprimanded by a mere amateur. Does he think they have just been weaned, taken off their mother's breast? What does he want with his baby-talk *saw lasaw* and *qaw laqaw*, sometimes here, sometimes there (v.10)? Whereas Klostermann assumes that Yahweh is being asked "whether he wants to move his instruction to the small children's room" (p. 214), modern commentators agree at least so far that it is the drunken priests who, with *saw lasaw* and *qaw laqaw* are imitating Isaiah's speech.

There is no problem in conceding to Klostermann that *saw lasaw* and *qaw laqaw* represent instruction of small children in the art of writing.[6] *Saw* stands for *sadeh* and *qaw* for *qoph*. The teacher, according to Klostermann, accommodates himself to the speech of small children. "The teacher is using a language despised by adults, but understood by the little ones who through it are helped to achieve knowledge" (p. 214).

Although we agree with Klostermann's interpretation of the *saw lasaw/qaw laqaw*, it must be said that he contradicts himself in another respect: do children who have just been weaned, i.e. those who are no more than three years old, have a teacher? Of course, not! It is the parents, in ancient Israel as well as among ourselves, who are using baby talk for the instruction of children of this age group. As far as we know, the education of the 3-5 age group was in Israel predominantly the father's responsibility. V.10a does, therefore, quite obviously not refer to a school situation.

The same applies to *ze'er sham ze'er sham*. According to KBL (3rd edition) *ze'er* means here 'a little'. O. Procksch[7] wants to read a school situation into our text and translate 'little one here, little one there!'.But there is no

(5)   G. Fohrer, *Das Buch Jesaja 2* (Zürich, 1962), p. 49.
(6)   Other possibilities of interpretation are listed by Fohrer, p. 51, note 44.
(7)   *Jesaja I* (Leipzig, 1930), ad loc.

philological evidence for such a translation.[8] Driver[9] is guilty of the same circular argument. His emendation - changing *sham* in v.10b into *sim* 'little one, pay attention!' - is already presupposing the school hypothesis, and, therefore, it cannot be used in evidence for it.

We, therefore, have to insist that Klostermann's second proof text also does not provide the necessary evidence: Isa. 28.10 refers solely to the education of small children by their parents, and not to a school.

This brings us to Klostermann's last piece of evidence, the third Servant Song in Isa. 50.4-9. What relevance this exilic text has for pre-exilic Israel, is a question which Klostermann never aks himself. It is *leshon limmudim* in v.4a which for Klostermann provides a link with a school situation. He concludes: "The prophet has before him from everyday life the picture of a school whose master uses the well trained pupils to instruct the beginners. He tells them the tasks and the methods of their solution, and they in turn, by setting an example and assisting, are meant to encourage the inexperienced pupils to try for themselves and gradually achieve success" (p. 213f).

According to KBL (3rd edn) and Gesenius-Buhl *limmud* means, firstly, as an adjective, 'used to something, practised in something' and, secondly, as a noun, 'pupil, disciple'. KBL derives Isa. 50.4 from the noun, 'a tongue of pupils', Gesenius-Buhl, however, from the adjective 'a tongue of practised ones', i.e. 'a practised tongue'. Because of the plural, *limmudim*, I regard this latter solution as the better one. This translation would already eliminate the school hypothesis. But let us, for this moment, use a neutral translation: 'Adonai Yahweh has given me a disciple tongue'.

Isa. 50.4-9 speaks of prophetic discipleship, first of all in relation to Yahweh: "It describes the Servant ... as a prophetic disciple, equipped and inspired by Yahweh".[10] "The prophet calls himself a disciple of God".[11] "The speaker in vv. 4-9 begins by saying that Yahweh has given him a disciplined tongue or ear, and he asserts that he has not been disobedient to his divine commission".[12]

The discipleship, secondly, refers to a prophetic chain of tradition: The Servant understands "his commission, his suffering, and his relation to God as part of a chain of prophets".[13] J.L.McKenzie refers to a "school of disciples

(8) Cf. Fohrer ad loc.
(9) *Semitic Writing from Pictograph to Alphabet* (2nd edn, London, 1954), note 1. Now in 3rd edn (1976).
(10) B.Duhm, *Das Buch Jesaja* (Göttingen, 5th edn 1968 = 4th edn 1922), p. 379.
(11) Fohrer, vol. 3 (1964), ad loc.
(12) C.R.North, *The Second Isaiah* (Oxford, 1964), ad loc.
(13) C.Westermann, *Jesaja 40-66* (Göttingen, 1966), ad loc.

which became a tradition, a tradition which the authors of Second Isaiah and Third Isaiah knew themselves to be continuators".[14]

If this third Servant Song refers to prophetic discipleship and not to the pupils of a school, we are forced to conclude in summary that in no case has Klostermann been able to prove the existence of schools in pre-exilic Israel.

The first proper investigation of the educational system in Israel and in the ancient Near East was carried out by Lorenz Dürr.[15] In the first two chapters of his book Dürr provides evidence for the existence of schools in Egypt on the one hand, and in Babylon and Assyria on the other. There is also some evidence for post-exilic Judaism: The term *talemid* appears for the first time in I Chron. 25.8.[16] The first mention of a school is in Sir. 51.23. The synagogue comes into existence, and in the 1st century A.D. we find public parochial schools and general school education.

For *pre*-exilic Israel, however, Dürr relies purely on Klostermann's results and does not add any new arguments. He also does not seem to be aware of the fact that, while he has plenty of evidence for Egypt, Babylon, and Assyria, this is not the case in the Old Testament. This should have made him reconsider his case.

It is in Dürr's book that we find the method of argumentation that was to become characteristic of future scholarship. One relies on the Egyptian and Mesopotamian parallels (argument by analogy), sometimes also on rabbinical material, and one closes the gap of evidence in the Old Testament by quoting Klostermann's hypotheses. But, as Klostermann could not provide sufficient evidence for his claims, this method has to be rejected.

It has frequently been claimed that the court of David and Solomon had special schools for the training of civil servants. As it so happens, we are very well informed indeed about David's and Solomon's administration. David had, according to II Sam. 8.15-18 (cf. I Chron. 18.14-17) and II Sam. 20.23-26, seven chief officers: the speaker or chancellor *mazkir*, the scribe or recorder *sopher*, the Commander in Chief of the army '*al-hassaba*', the commander of the mercenaries '*al-hakkereti wehappeleti*,[17] the officer in charge of forced labour '*al-hammas*, and two priests *kohanim*. David's sons probably belonged to the throne council as ministers without portfolio,

---

(14) *Second Isaiah* (Garden City, New York, 1968), p. 116f.

(15) *Das Erziehungswesen im AT und im antiken Orient* (Leipzig, 1932).

(16) This, however, applies to musicians and probably presupposes the circumstances of the time of the Chronicler rather than those of the time of David.

(17) He was perhaps subject to the Commander in Chief of the army, because in II Sam. 20.23a the latter is specifically referred to as '*al kol-hassaba*'.

because in II Sam. 8.18b they appear as *kohanim*, but in I Chron. 18.17b, perhaps more correctly, as *harishonim leyad hammelek*.

Solomon, according to I Kings 4.2-6, retained the positions of these chief officers, with the exception of that of the commander of the mercenaries. His function was absorbed by the Commander in Chief of the army. In addition, Solomon's complex administration demanded a second *sopher*, a minister *'al-hannisabim* who was the head of the twelve officers,[18] and a chamberlain *'al-habbayit*. New also is the office of the 'King's friend' *re'eh hammelek* and the position of the high priest, *hakkohen*, made necessary by the building of the temple. Thus, in Solomon's throne council we find eleven chief officers, but there is no head of the school *'al-bet hassepher* or *'al-bet hammiderash*.

Archaeology, too, makes the argument from silence more and more difficult. Excavations in Israel have progressed so far that we could expect material comparable to that from Egypt and Mesopotamia, had there been schools in Israel during the monarchy.– Lemaire, in his new book, is in fact trying to argue from archaeological evidence.[19] – For Solomon's supply and military policy archaeology has been very helpful.[20]

As the scribal office was hereditary, schools for training were unnecessary: Elihoreph and Ahija, Solomon's scribes (I Kings 4.3), were the sons of Shisha who held the same office under David.[21] The family of the scribe Shaphan, who is mentioned in connection with Josiah's law-book in II Kings 22, seems to have held similar positions under Josiah's son, Jehoiakim. We hear of Shaphan's son Ahikam (Jer. 26.24), Gemariah and his grandson Michaiah (both in Jer. 36.9-13). Whereas Shisha's and Shaphan's families were distinguished royal officers, the scribal families of Jabez (I Chron. 2.55)

(18) Cf. I Kings 4.7-19.

(19) A.Lemaire, *Les écoles et la formation de la Bible dans l'ancient Israel* (Freiburg/Schweiz and Göttingen, 1981), points to isolated epigraphic material from 'Izbeth Sartah, Gezer, Lachish, Khirbet 'el-Qom, Arad, Aroer and Qadesh-Barnea which might represent pupils' writing exercises. He himself refers to these findings as "très pauvre et très fragmentaire" (p. 84). But in no case is Lemaire able to prove that these findings derive from a school rather than from private instruction on the basis of the famulus system. Had all this material been found in one place, particularly in Jerusalem, one would be more inclined to think of a school.

(20) Cf. the articles in M.Avi-Yonah (ed), *Encyclopedia of Archaeological Excavations in the Holy Land 2* (London, 1976): "Gezer", pp. 428-43; "Hazor", pp. 474-95; "Jerusalem", pp. 579-647; and vol. 3 (ed. by Avi-Yonah and E.Stern, 1977): "Megiddo", pp. 830-56.

(21) The identity of Shisha with the Sheja or Shewa of II Sam. 20.25 or with the Shawsha of I Chron. 18.16 is now generally accepted in the commentaries.

seem to have pursued more humble occupations.

If one denies the existence of schools in pre-exilic Israel, one has to answer the question in what way people were educated. How, e.g., was reading and writing taught? The idea of turning to Egypt for analogies is not as bad as it may sound. We only have to consider very carefully what actually can be compared, i.e. where do we find genuine analogies?

There are two possible approaches to which I shall refer as *chronological* and *sociological* comparison. Scholarship today uses almost exclusively the first method. One compares the institutions of the Israelite monarchy with its *chronological* Egyptian counterpart, the late period of the Egyptian empire, from the 21st to the 26th dynasty (1085-527).[22] The Middle and the New Kingdom, however, are still considered as background. This method leads inevitably to the claim of the existence of schools in Israel, as they can be found in Egypt since the Middle Kingdom. This approach is based on a fallacy when comparing Egyptian and Israelite institutions. Whereas in Egypt during the Middle Kingdom, New Kingdom, and the late period we are confronted with a highly developed empire, Israel at the time of David and Solomon is still at her very beginnings. That implies that Egyptian institutions can only be assumed to have existed in Israel at the same time, if we have positive evidence.[23]

At this point the *sociological* approach, which compares similar societies, is more helpful. The Egyptian counterpart to the early Israelite monarchy is the Old Kingdom. When two societies have reached a similar stage of development, we find many analogies between them. So, we are not surprised to learn that there were no schools in the Old Kingdom.[24] Using this analogy, one would then not postulate them for Israel without positive evidence.

Helmuth Brunner[25] the famous Tübingen Egyptologist, describes the educational system and the training of civil servants in the Old Kingdom as follows: Education presupposes a so-called master-apprentice system ("Magister-Famulussystem"). This system corresponds roughly to the

---

(22) For the Egyptian chronology I follow E.Otto, *Ägypten - Der Weg des Pharaonenreiches* (Stuttgart, 2nd edn 1955).

(23) According to D.B.Redford, "Studies in relations between Palestine and Egypt during the First Millennium B.C.", in: J.W.Wevers and D.B.Redford (eds), *Studies in the Ancient Palestinian World* (Toronto, 1971), pp. 141-56, Solomon has taken over the Egyptian fiscal system, but not Egypt's governmental offices.

(24) H.Brunner, *Altägyptische Erziehung* (Wiesbaden, 1957), p. 10.

(25) op.cit., p. 10f.

master-apprentice system used by the medieval German craftsmen. A wise and experienced civil servant accepts a pupil into his household and educates him. These pupils are known as 'sons'. The adopted 'son' is often held up as an example to the scribe's own bodily son. According to Brunner, the continuity of Egyptian society is based on this apprentice system. It would appear that already elementary instruction in reading and writing was given on this basis in the Old Kingdom.

This *sociological* comparison of the early Israelite monarchy with the Old Kingdom in Egypt agrees much better with the picture provided for this period by the Old Testament. The best explanation for the fact that no schools are mentioned is still that there were none! The education of the Israelite boy, after he has been weaned, is his father's responsibility. Even more so than in the Old Kingdom in Egypt, Israelite boys have almost without exception taken up their fathers' profession, particularly priests and scribes. Even Jesus is still learning the carpenter's trade. In Israel, therefore, one's own son is normally identical with one's pupil, and the art of reading and writing is being transmitted in this way, just like all other professional skills (against von Rad).

If the Israelite boy wanted to or was intended to pursue a profession different from that of his father, Israel was quite well acquainted with the master-apprentice system. We see it at work in the case of young Samuel's education in the house of Eli (I Sam. 1). Here, too, we find the contrast, familiar from the Old Kingdom in Egypt, between the wicked sons of Eli and the well-behaved apprentice, Samuel (I Sam. 2).

Furthermore, it seems to have been David's policy to leave intact the native administration in Jerusalem and other occupied territories. There was, therefore, no necessity to create, practically overnight, a large and complex administration. The Israelite civil service was therefore able to develop gradually by relying on family tradition and the apprentice system. In this case, the hypothesis of the existence of schools because of the complexities of the administration becomes redundant.

That the question of the existence of schools in pre-exilic Israel is important for scholars' judgment of Wisdom *in general* can be shown clearly in von Rad's case, who also considerably changes his position between the *Theology*[26] and *Wisdom in Israel*.[27]

In the *Theology* (vol.1, p.430ff.) von Rad does not regard Wisdom as primarily didactic. The origin of Wisdom for him has to do with the finding

---

(26) *Theologie des Alten Testaments*, vol.1 (München, 6th edn 1969 = 4th edn 1962).

(27) *Weisheit in Israel* (Neukirchen-Vluyn, 1970).

of order and the security of life. Wisdom represents the empirical and gnomic approach to truth - as opposed to the systematic one in theology and philosophy.

Von Rad distinguishes between the actual *proverb* on the one hand, and the *aphorism* or *epigram* on the other. Only when trying to determine the life situation *of the latter* as a work of art, he refers to the cultivation of Wisdom at the Israelite Royal Court. Israelite Wisdom for von Rad is not half as much attached to a particular class or the world of the civil servant as that of Egypt (p. 443).

Von Rad reckons with a broad base of *popular proverbs* in Prov., although these have, no doubt, been collected at the royal court in Jerusalem. When popular proverbs are being used as educational wisdom for the training of civil servants, he regards this as a *secondary usage*.[28] We may therefore conclude that von Rad's understanding of the relationship between popular and educational wisdom is still well balanced in the *Theology*. He emphasizes the difference between Egypt and Israel.

In *Wisdom in Israel*, however, he abandons the quest for the pre-history of the Book of Proverbs as "meaningless". He argues consistently from literary wisdom which he understands as school wisdom. He does not deny the existence of an older popular wisdom on principle, but it has become "a phenomenon difficult to define." (p.24). Von Rad justifies his understanding of Wisdom as court wisdom with the allusion to Solomon and the *analogy* with Egypt and Mesopotamia (p.28). Although von Rad admits that the majority of the proverbs has nothing to do with the Court, his bourgeois prejudice forces him to attribute them in that case to the *upper classes of the bourgeoisie* and the gentlemen farmers (p. 30f.). That way he can still consider them educational, and not popular wisdom.

The existence of schools follows for von Rad simply from the fact that writing was practised in Israel. He tells the surprised reader: "All writing had to be taught. But writing was never taught without doctrine or instruction which formed part of it. Consequently, there must have been schools of various kinds in Israel"(p. 31). So simple is all this! The Book of Proverbs now has to be considered as poetry. The formerly widespread opinion - indeed shared by von Rad himself - that we are dealing with popular proverbs he now rejects by quoting his pupil H.-J. Hermisson.[29]

---

(28) Likewise C.Westermann, "Weisheit im Sprichwort", *Forschung am Alten Testament 2* (München, 1974), pp. 149-61.

(29) Von Rad, *Weisheit in Israel*, p. 42, on H.-J. Hermisson, *Studien zur israelitischen Spruchweisheit* (Neukirchen-Vluyn, 1968), p.52ff.

In summary: Von Rad abandons the question of popular wisdom, which he had still pursued in the *Theology* as meaningless in *Wisdom in Israel*. He now exclusively understands Wisdom as school wisdom or educational wisdom of the early monarchy. Where *court* origin is absolutely impossible or unlikely, the educated bourgeoisie has to take its place. The difference between Egyptian and Israelite wisdom, which he used to emphasize, he now down-grades. I strongly suspect that the change in von Rad's opinion is, in both cases, due to the influence of his pupil, Hermisson.

Hermisson himself considers proverbial wisdom purely as *literature*. He finds the place of origin and transmission of proverbs in a class of educated people, who as teachers and pupils belonged to the Israelite school for civil servants (p.188). Two things are, according to Hermisson, characteristic of the Wisdom of the early monarchy: Firstly, its centre was the Israelite school, and, secondly, it was the education, art and science of an epoch long past (p. 192).

Hermisson reaches these results in an astonishing way. Every unbiased reader would naturally assume that proverbs have originated among ordinary people and that a different kind of origin would need explaining. Hermisson, however, offers the methodical instruction that "*not the origin of proverbs among wise men, but the origin of proverbs among the people needs proving*" (sic!) (p. 25). With this presupposition, Hermisson is no longer troubled by the contrary evidence of Prov. 10-29: "Of course, these sayings are formulated in a very general sense. But, in no case is one actually *forced* to assume origin among the people, because the content of these sayings applies also - often especially - to the upper classes" (p. 76).

Hermisson's view of Israelite wisdom rests on two main presuppositions:

(1) The assumption of a class of 'wise men' in Israel, and

(2) his claim that schools existed in Israel during the early monarchy.

(ad 1) That the *hakamim* were no professional class, like the *kohanim* and *nebi'im*, has already been proved by R.N. Whybray.[30] I have nothing to add to his arguments. But, it is about time that scholars, particularly in Germany, took note of them.

(ad 2) The existence of schools for the monarchical period is still

(30) *The Intellectual Tradition in the Old Testament*, BZAW 135 (Berlin and New York, 1974), pp. 15-54. This applies, according to Whybray, even to Jer. 18.18: "the triple saying is not, as is generally believed, a reference to three professional classes who form the mainstay of the Judaean state. It is simply a contemptuous reference to three kinds of people whose common characteristic is that they are for ever talking, but whose talk is valueless. They are '*aneshe sephatayim*'" (p.31).

unproven. This has been extensively pointed out by Whybray (pp. 33-43). But as he is concerned with later literary wisdom, he did not realise the significance of his own observations with regard to the *origin* of Wisdom.

There is, therefore, no evidence for the derivation of Wisdom from Israel's schools which Hermisson claims, because it is based on two presuppositions which are in turn unproven. The origin of proverbs among ordinary people is still more likely. Hermisson's investigations seem to me to be hindered by a bourgeois-elitist concept of education. He has to deny the existence of any folk wisdom, so that it can instead be attributed to the creative individual personality. The origin of this way of thinking in 19th century German idealism is self-evident.

That with the wisdom school hypothesis we are not dealing with a minor error, but with a whole branch of scholarship moving blindly into the wrong direction, can be shown from Udo Skladny's careful study of Prov. 10ff, *Die ältesten Spruchsammlungen in Israel* (Göttingen, 1962). In his case, the complete operational blindness of Old Testament scholarship in the question of the origin of Wisdom becomes sadly obvious. Skladny recognizes Prov. 25-27 (= collection C) as applying to farmers and craftsmen. As such, he would have to date them early on the basis of his own results. But the Court/school hypothesis forces him to declare that we are dealing with an adjustment of Court Wisdom to the lower levels of society. That these lower levels of society, peasants and craftsmen, could have produced folk wisdom themselves has become an inconceivable idea.

In consequence Skladny is forced to stand his relative chronology on its head and to regard Prov. 25-27 as late: "Against regarding collection C as the oldest composition advises its contents, adjusted to peasants and farmers. Because *either* one would have to look for the origin of Wisdom *outside* the royal court which is unlikely, because of the close connection between Wisdom and court – *or* one would have to assume that Wisdom formerly addressed itself to a circle of ordinary people far from the court (rather than to the scribe or the ruler) – a similarly absurd suggestion" (p.77). The criticism of this position comes from no Old Testament scholar, but from the German poet, Christian Morgenstern:

"Weil, so schließt er messerscharf
nicht sein kann, was nicht sein darf." (Palmström)
(Because, so he concludes with the sharpness of a knife's
edge, what must not be, cannot be!)

Having recognized this desolate state of affairs in our discipline, I should like to propose a twofold remedy:

(1) Negative: We have to take seriously Whybray's criticism of the unproven hypotheses ('class of wise men', 'schools') and base our arguments solely on the Old Testament evidence.

(2) Positive: The question of an indigenous Israelite popular wisdom, suppressed by Hermisson and the later von Rad, has to be asked again.[31] It is on this second point that, following an article by Claus Westermann[32] which has been totally ignored, I should wish to put forward the following seven theses:

(I) A proverb has to be explained *primarily* from its life situation, and only *secondarily* from its literary context.

(II) The genre of the proverb occurs among *illiterate* peoples.

(III) To start with, *all* wisdom is expressed through proverbs; there are no other forms of expression as yet.[33]

(IV) The Old Testament and the other highly developed civilizations represent a late stage of the genre 'proverb' which is actually alive in tribal cultures.

(V) This would have to be proved by a representative survey of proverbs of tribal cultures.[34]

(VI) If the aspects of life depicted in the Israelite proverbs and those of tribal societies are basically the same, then the derivation of Hebrew wisdom from Egypt and Mesopotamia is in doubt. It would then have to be explained as indigenous wisdom.

(VII) This indigenous Israelite wisdom might turn out to be older than commonly assumed and might go back to the early history of the tribes.

---

(31) That the Egyptian parallels have to be considered together with the later Hebrew instructions is not a point at issue.

(32) "Weisheit im Sprichwort", see note 28.

(33) I refer to the Sumerian proverbs, which have probably been collected around 3000 B.C., and to those of tribal cultures.

(34) Hermisson, pp. 81-92, has rightly rejected the idea of a nomadic clan wisdom. We shall have to think of sedentary farmers as those who produce proverbs.

2

The Royal and Court Sayings and the Origin of Israelite Wisdom

Our research into Israelite Wisdom has in my opinion reached its third phase. First of all Wisdom was mistakenly considered a purely post-exilic form of thought, based on the dogma of retribution. This evaluation was rectified during the second phase, as it became clear through comparison with Egypt and Mesopotamia that Wisdom thought is considerably earlier. Now we have entered, according to G. von Rad,[1] into the third phase of research which is more and more concerned with finding out what is specific to Israel's Wisdom as opposed to that of the Ancient Near East.

When inquiring into the origin of indigenous Israelite Wisdom, one quickly discovers that it is still the hypotheses of phase II which determine our research, viz. the school hypothesis and the royal court hypothesis. These in my opinion prevent a priori the quest for the specific character of Israelite Wisdom, as demanded by G. von Rad. If we continue to regard Israel's Wisdom through Egyptian spectacles, its indigenous features are unlikely to become much clearer. I have already attempted to show elsewhere that Israel had no schools during the period of the monarchy and that the training of scribes occurred as family tradition or through a tutorial system.[2] In this paper I shall be attempting to refute the second hypothesis, viz. that Wisdom has its origins in the royal court and that it is based on the ethics of the civil service. I am not denying that proverbs were collected at court – where else? (Cf. Prov 25.1). I, therefore, must emphasize that I am not discussing the collection or redaction of proverbs, but the question of their origin.

(1) *Weisheit in Israel* (Neukirchen-Vluyn, 1970), p.20-3,
(2) "Die israelitische Weisheitsschule oder 'Des Kaisers neue Kleider'", *VT* 33 (1983), p. 257-70.

16

I intend to refute the royal court hypothesis with an investigation of the royal and court sayings in Prov 10 - 29. It is generally taken for granted that the mere mention of the king is an indication that the proverb in question originated at the royal court. The classic representative of this position is H.-J. Hermisson:

"With the royal sayings we can deal quickly, because *their popular origin is quite inconceivable*. While theoretically popular imagination might have been attracted by the court and thus might have produced proverbs, the royal sayings in Prov. are not of this kind."[3]

Our task can be divided into two parts: (I) Through the use of African parallels I intend to prove the existence of royal and court sayings coined by circles which are themselves socially distant from the king or chief (Volksmund, ordinary people). This will be followed (II) by the question, whether the royal and court sayings contained in the oldest collections Prov 10 - 29 originated at the court itself or among ordinary people.

(I) African Proverbs

(1) *Proverbs Critical of the King or Chief* [4]

With this group it is easiest to demonstrate that criticism of the chief or king must have arisen in circles which were themselves distant from the court. A large number of these proverbs deal with the equality of all men, which, of course, includes the chief and his advisers:

Mal. 849 "All people are like with you in possessing three posts" (= "to support the roof of the native house").[5] Mal. 1386 "The great are open to

---

(3) *Studien zur israelitischen Spruchweisheit* (Neukirchen-Vluyn, 1968), p. 71.

(4) The expression "critical of the king" has been taken from F. Crüsemann, *Der Widerstand gegen das Königtum. Die antiköniglichen Texte des AT*...(Neukirchen-Vluyn, 1978). As far as I know, Crüsemann is the first Old Testament scholar who has used comparative material from Affical tribal societies and has shown these to be comparable to the Israel of the time of the Judges. African proverbs talk mostly about the chief, often about the king, and sometimes about the sovereign. The transition is a fluent one. This is also the case in the Old Testament. The role of Saul is similar to that of an African chief, and David begins his rise even lower down, viz. as a brigand.

(5) J.A. Houlder, *OHABOLANA or Malagasy Proverbs I and II* (Antananarivo, 1915/16); French translations by H. Noyer (= Mal.). The explanations given by the original collectors and editors are quoted in brackets (= ...).

shame / and the small are open to fear."[6] Mal. 1421 "A canoe is not partial
to a prince / whoever is upset gets wet." - The chief has no privilege. While
he may be economically better off than his people, death makes everybody
equal: Ton. 265 "Hunger does not enter the chief's home / but death does."[7]
The Kafir have a similar saying: Kaf. (2), p. 297 "Death does not know
Kings."[8]

Ton. 265 "Woman has no chief." (= "A chief is no chief to his wife.")
At home the great chief turns out to be a henpecked husband. A nice
example of popular humour. In our society, too, jokes are used by ordinary
people as a means of fighting those in power. The Baganda, too, remind their
chief that all people are equal: Bag. p. 489 "The drum beats for the office
/ and not for the person who holds it."[9]

A group of sayings describes the *dependence of the chief on his people*: Ton.
4 "The elephant is the trunk." ("Without its trunk, the elephant cannot seize
anything. Without his subjects, a chief cannot do his work.") In many
proverbs the elephant represents the chief. Ton. 246 "The centipede's legs
are strengthened by a hundred rings." (= A chief's strength lies in the number
of his subjects.") Ton. 269 "People are wealth." (= "People whom you
govern ... are the basis of your power.").- As in Ton. 4 the chief is being
confronted with the fact that the people are the real basis of his power.
Without his subjects the chief is nothing. Like the Tonga, the Fante, p. 518,
regard the people as power base: "If Otsibo says he can do something / he
does it with his followers."[10] The next Fante proverbs has the same
significance (ibid.): "Though the elephant is huge / his domain is looked
after by the duiker (African gazelle)".

The following proverbs put the *people above the chief*: Mal. 1414 "Better
be hated by the prince / than hated by the people" (= "intercession
possible").- Mal. 1417 "A poor prince is not equal to a rich commoner."-
This proverbs puts wealth above chieftaincy, but often the opposite view is
taken, e.g. by the Lovedu (see below). The Fante, too, put the people clearly

---

(6) I quote these proverbs in units of meaning without commata, as we are dealing with
oral literature (Cf. Ruth Finnegan, *Oral Literature in Africa* [Oxford, 1970], dividing
sections by (/). Proverbs are handed on orally in Africa. The written collections have
been assembled by European missionaries, anthropologists etc.

(7) H.P.Junod and A.A.Jaques, *The Wisdom of the Tonga-Shangaan People* (Cleveland,
Transvaal, 1936) (= Ton.).

(8) Dudley Kidd, *The Essential Kafir* (London, 1904) (= Kaf.2).

(9) John Roscoe, *The Baganda* (London, 1911) (= Bag).

(10) J.B. Christensen, "The Role of Proverbs in Fante Culture", in E.P. Skinner (ed.),
Peoples and Cultures of Africa (New York, 1973), p. 509ff. (= Fante).

above the chief (p. 518): "Though the coconut tree is smooth / the palm-nut tree is king." (= The palm-nut tree is likened to the people because of its many products.")

A fourth group describes the *transitoriness of power.* Ton. 107 and the Bantu[11] (p. 48): "Authority (power) is the tail of the water-rat." (= A chief's power slips away from the one who possesses it. If you try to catch a water-rat, its tail remains in your hand, while the rat escapes.")- The Mashona[12] (p. 175) compare the transitoriness of chieftaincy to the dew: "Dew soon dries up / so will chieftaincy."- Also the Lunda[13] (p. 282) warn their chief: "The talking bird was master / he scattered his following." (= A headman ... who nags will soon find himself alone.") - And also the Akikuyu know (Aki.,[14] p.224) how easily a chief can lose his power: "A potent man does not insult two seasons.- Cf. the German "Hochmut kommt vor dem Fall."

The next group deals with the *removal of the chief;* in these proverbs the democratic element is very prominent: Mal. 1420 "A sovereign too gentle has no kingdom / a sovereign too severe does not dwell with his subjects." (= "In either case they relieve themselves of his services.") - A dangerous chief who turns on his own subjects is being removed by the Fante (p. 518): "If you see a stick that will pierce your eye / break it off" (= "removal of a chief"). - And in bad times the Fante chief who has lost his charisma and his popularity is being got at (ibid): "The throat that gulps down good soup / is the very throat that receives the bullet in time of difficulty." - A chief lives dangerously.

Some proverbs describe *the little man's fear of the chief.* Mal. 1399 "The sovereign is like fire: / if you go far off / you get cold / and if you come near / you get burned." - Ton. 130 "Do not open the mouth of the roaring bull." ("Do not speak with the angry chief.") - A trivial warning for civil servants, but a matter of life and death for ordinary people! Ton. 255 "Authority has no sweetness." (= "A chief seldom pays attention to a poor man's misfortune.") - A typical poor man's complaint about the chief. - The Fante (p. 518) warn the small man: "One does not state what one thinks in front of a chief / but behind his back." - A civil servant would know this anyway. The small man's fear of the chief is also reflected by another Fante proverb (ibid): "The chief has ears / like those of an elephant."-

(11) H.P.Junod, *Bantu Heritage* (Johannesburg, 1938), p. 46ff. (= Bantu).

(12) C. Bullock, *The Mashona. The Indigenous Natives of S. Rhodesia* (Cape Town and Johannesburg, 1927) (= Mash.).

(13) F.H. Melland, *In Witch-bound Africa* (London, 1923) (= Lunda).

(14) C. Cagnolo, *The Akikuyu. Their Customs, Traditions and Folklore* (Nyeri/Kenya, 1933), p. 214ff. (= Aki.).

The German "Gehe nie zu deinem Fürst / wenn du nicht gerufen wirst" can be found among the Chagga[15] (Chag.13): "Those who come early / and those who go late to the chief / find a dead dog." (= It is better to stay at home and to mind your own business than to idle around the Chief's residence, where you are likely to be involved in strife, and where many are killed.") – In this case the speakers are small people who have had bad experiences with the chief and those surrounding him, and no courtiers!

The following sayings deal with *the people's dependence on their chief:* Mal. 1416 "An ox does not refuse his lot / a Hova does not choose his sovereign." – The Hova (lower class) has no choice of his master. The latter is imposed upon him like a burden on an ox.– Many peoples attribute their mistakes to the bad example of the chief: Mal. 1638 "If the headmen are foolish / the people are also foolish." Similarly Ton. 261 "When the chief limps / all his subjects limp also." (= "If a chief or leader is not honest, those who follow him will not be honest either."). – Also Ton. 262 "If the leader does not walk straight / those who follow him do the same."

The following are examples of sayings which express *hatred* and *threats* of the people against the chief: Mal. 1428 "The mist rests in the valleys / the crocodiles lie in the streams / the lowly hate the lofty." – This proverb regards three things as self-evident: fog in the valleys, crocodiles in rivers, and the hatred of the ordinary people against their rulers. Such realism you would hardly expect in court wisdom. Even without an introduction we recognize the structure of a numerical saying $x/x+1$.[16] Ton. 44 "Do not whirl a snake in the air / when you have killed it / the ones which remain in their holes / see you." (= Said to a chief who deals very harshly with a poor person.") – The large number of the people has the longer breath and threatens the chief with retribution.

Some proverbs are directed against too much *submissiveness*: Ton. 72 "You cannot dig up the hole of the ant-eater / but you may peep into it." (= "The chief cannot be forced to do anything, but you may question him without causing offence.") – Subjects, do not give up immediately! – Ton. 286 "A man who has paid his tribute to the chief / is not afraid." – The small man who has paid up on time does not have to crawl before the chief.

Some sayings counsel the chief to use *persuasion* rather than authority: Mal. 1404 "Don't say: Mine is the word / for I am king." – The king is to use his authority cautiously. – Mal. 140 "A word (well) discussed makes the

---

(15) C. Dundas, *Kilimanjaro and its People* (London, 1924), p. 341ff. (= Chag.).
(16) W.M.W. Roth, "The Numerical Sequence x/x+1 in the OT", *VT* 12 (1962), p. 300-
    11.

sovereign powerful" (= affermit l'autorité du souverain"). - The chief is meant to convince and not to enforce. - Ton. 260 "Take care of it / it will take care of you." (= "Take care of your people, and they will take care of you. Said in criticism of a chief who applies the law too harshly to a poor subject.") - As this proverb can also apply to father and child, it is suggested to the chief that he should regard himself as a father of his people.

There is also a whole series of individual proverbs which treat the chief critically: Mal. 1418 "Like demanding payment of debt from a prince / it is the creditor that does the coaxing." - The chiefs do not even want to pay their debts.

Ton. 253 points out the limits of the chief's authority: "The authority (of a chief) does not cross the river." (= "A chief's power does not function outside his own country.")

A hesitant chief is attacked by the people by means of satire: Ton. 254 "Authority has no skin." (= "As the leopards and lions, kings of beasts, always fight, their skin is not in good condition. It has holes or is often scratched. This proverb satirizes a chief who is afraid to give a definite decision in a case.") The complete helplessness of ordinary people in relation to the chief is descibed by Ton. 258 "Greatness buys." (= "A poor man, even though he sees a chief doing wrong, has no right to reprimand the chief, or to dispute with him.") - Similarly Ton. 259 "The chief's trumpet never refuses to blow." (= "The chief's words are always orders, and they must always be obeyed.") It does not matter whether you like it or not!

But even the chief's favour is a double-edged sword for the small man, as it makes his social equals suspicious: Chag. 16 "If the chief gives you a ring / hide it in your clothing." (= "Do not let men see that you are distinguished.")

Summarising I/1 we may conclude that in the African proverbs critical of king or chief ordinary people express their worries about their ruler. While the proverbs describe on the negative side the people's fear of the chief and their dependence on him, on the positive side they emphasize the equality of all men and encourage the honest citizen not to crawl before the chief. The reason for this is simply that the chief in turn is dependent on his people. The democratic element is particularly strong in those sayings which advise the chief not to go too far, and in those that call for the removal of a tyrant.

(2) *Proverbs critical of the court*

That the following are popular sayings is clear from the fact that the very courtiers, to whom the origin of wisdom in Israel is so often attributed, appear to be their favourite targets.

A courtier's position is, in the people's opinion, nothing special and its holder easily replaceable: Mal. 1438 "A horse of honours: dead today / it is substituted tomorrow" (= "high officer"). - According to the people, the chief's clientele only cling to him in order to attempt to profit from him: Mal.1440 "A weaver finch going with the cardinal-bird / it is not the leader / but simply goes together with it."

Courtiers *fallen from grace* are mocked: Mal. 1484 "Raised up to let fall / like a mallet." (= "Said mockingly of the fallen.")

According to the Malagasy there is a *difference* in principle between the chief and the courtier: Mal. 1485 "The cock and the sun / they make an appointment (i.e. to rise betimes in the morning) / but they are far away from each other."

And the same people say to officials who *abuse their power.* Mal. 2252 "Don't issue orders without your superior's consent!" - The Tonga-Shanga do not like to deal with subordinates and say: Ton. 23 "It is those in front who ask about the buffalo." (= "A difficult case must be dealt with by people in authority, who lead others.")

Typical of the civil servants' *behaviour* is the following proverb: Ton. 81 (= Bantu, p. 47) "Once a baboon has tasted honey / it does not touch earth again." (= "Once a man has been put in a position of authority, he does not accept an inferior one.") - Among the Fante (p. 513) the chief's mistakes are often passed off as those of his messengers: "There are no bad chiefs / only bad messengers." - The chief's spokesmen are very important in the political system of the Fante.

The Akikuyu put the *chief above his courtiers*: Aki., p. 233 "The eyes of the frog do not prevent the cattle drinking." (Cf. "The lion is not afraid of the jackal.") Among the Hausa[17] civil servants are not held in very high esteem: Hausa 44 "The eyes that beheld the chief / do not fear the galadima (a court official)."

And the Ovimbundu in Angola[18] criticize those people who have reached their positions through favouritism: Ovim., p. 253 "The turtle cannot climb up on a stump / someone has to put it there."

And the Hausa finally point out that the courtiers are *envious* of the chief:

(17) R.S. Rattray, *Hausa Folk-lore II* (Oxford, 1913), p. 254ff. (= Hausa).
(18) W.D. Hambly, *The Ovimbundu of Angola* (Chicago, 1934) (= Ovim.).

Hausa 59 "The leopard envies the lion's resting-place." - The privileges of the Hausa civil service, too, cannot be compared to those of the chief's family: Hausa 81 "Silver stirrups even at the chief's courtyard / it is the chief's son who has them." (= "There are plenty of rich and powerful people about, but none of them have the privilege of having silver stirrups.")

Our summary of I/2 shows clearly the unpopularity of civil servants and courtiers among the people. It is best to go straight to the chief, rather than dealing with his underlings. As the courtiers are very conceited, the people rejoice when the former fall from grace, especially as they have often reached their positions through favouritism rather than effort. Not only are the courtiers determined to hang on to these positions, but they are even envious of the chief. So we are not really surprised to find that the criticism of the courtiers can turn into a positive evaluation of the chief, as represented by the next group of proverbs.

(3) *Proverbs sympathetic to the chief*

A large number of proverbs conclude that one cannot serve two *masters* at the same time. These are expressions of a *conflict of loyalties* among the people, not the worries of a mole in the civil service: Ton. 13 (cf. Bantu, p. 47) "Two lions fear each other." (= "Two chiefs show respect to each other.") - This is noted by the people with surprise when they think of their own treatment by the chief. - Ton. 110 "Two squirrels do not remain in one hole"; and also Ton. 138 "Two bulls cannot be in the same kraal." (= "There cannot be two chiefs in the same country.") - This would lead to a conflict of loyalties for the people. - Mash., p. 175 "Two male mice do not live in one hole / one will come out with half a tail." - Ton. 266 "Two chiefs do not pay tribute to each other." (= "The sovereignty of the chief is absolute.") - Thus says the small man who unfortunately must himself pay. - The Ewe[19] express the problem of two masters either with or without the use of an image: Ewe 21 "Two kings do not rule in one town"; or Ewe 66 "Two big fish do not drink water in the hollow of one rock."

In the next group of proverbs the people recognize the chief's *function of order.* Fante, p. 518 "A snare is destroyed / when an elephant places his foot in it." (= "Plots against the chief are easily squashed.") - There is no point in an uprising. This saying contradicts some of the proverbs critical of the chief which suggest his removal from office. - Cf. also Fante (ibid): "A cow can only be tethered to a strong tree." (= "The chief can check even the strongest.") - The authority of the chief, against which there is no appeal, the Fante (ibid) describe as follows: "After the elephant (= chief) there is no

(19) A.B. Ellis, *The EWE-Speaking Peoples* (London, 1890) (= Ewe).

other animal." - Experience has shown that among the Lunda the lack of a chief leads to chaos: Lunda, p. 282 "The cock died in the village / the chicks remained clucking." (= "When there is no chief, there is no order in the village or country.")

Chag. 14 takes a similar view: "The bull that is slaughtered sighs: / I die - woe my skin." (= "When a great man dies - it may be a Chief - his dependents suffer..."). The Akikuyu know, too, that the tribe is helpless without a good leader: Aki., p. 214 "(The goats) having a lame leader / do not arrive at the grass." - The small people submit willingly to the chief: Aki., p. 224 "The neck does not grow over the head." - The chief's function of order is also known to the Hausa (15): "The cat is not at home / because of that the mice are playing."

The next group of sayings speaks of the chief's *glory* and his *mediation of blessing* for the people: Mal. 1399 "The sovereign is like the sky and cannot be measured / and like the sun and cannot be spanned (or opposed)." - The images of spacial distance hint at the social distance the speakers feel between themselves and their subject. A courtier would have been more likely to have "measured up" to his chief. - In the following proverb it is the people who in my opion place the chief above the great ones of the tribe: Mal. 1408 "The many are like the sovereign / the sovereign is a sovereign already!" - This is obviously an attack on those surrounding the chief. - Supporting the chief pays for the small man: Mal. 1413 "Watercourses are made to catch crabs / the earth is dug to get the avoko root / and the sovereign is followed to get meat" (soldiers' pay).

As the people derive their own stupidity from the chief (Mal. 1638), so also their own wisdom: Mal. 1639 "If the headmen are wise / the people are also wise." - Fante, p.518 "One cannot make the same tracks as an elephant (= chief)." - The people regard themselves as inferior to the chief. - (ibid.): "When you follow the elephant / you will not be ensnared in difficulties." - This sounds a bit like slavish obedience. - (ibid.): "When the chief's breast has plenty of milk / it is for all the world to drink." - The people regard the chief as mediator of blessing. Most interesting in this case is the use of the image of a mother or nurse for a male chief (cf. Numb. 11.12; Deut. 1.31). - The people demand leadership from the chief knowing that this is to their own benefit: Bantu, p. 48 "A dog's strength is for its master to set it hunting." (= "A subordinate is inefficient without his master's guidance.")

The Bavenda[20] recognize the superiority of the chief over his people:

(20) H.A. Stayt, *The Bavenda* (London, 1931), p. 360-1 (= Bav.).

Bav. 19 "The pot which is poured into / is better than that which is cooked."
- The Lovedu[21] have noticed that the rain-maker is powerless without the chief: "If the chief holds the rain from falling / the doctor cannot cause rain."

Their knowledge that royal rank is something special is expressed by the Lovedu in two proverbs (p. 287): "Robes may be passed on (to strangers) / never royal rank;" and (ibid.) "What becomes worn by age is clothes / not noble rank." - The Bechuana[22] regard the chief as the executor of the will of God: Bech., p. 202 "God is (generally) on the side of the chief." - Like the Fante (supra) the Chagga also describe the chief as mediator of blessing by using female images: Chag. 17 "But one bull in the land / gave milk for all the women." - The trust of ordinary Chagga people in their chief as helper in need is reflected in Chag. 17a: "If the cattle are finished / yet have we a chief." (= "So long as the country was not without a ruler, its fortunes could be restored.") - Ewe 102 "The big water-pot goes not to the well." - As the big water-pot does not go the well itself, but is filled by others, so the small people serve the chief.

The chief's *justice* is the topic of a further group of proverbs: Bantu, p. 48 "The chief has no relative." (= "When you have committed an offence, do not trust that the chief will acquit you because you are related to him.") - The Baganda regard their king as absolutely impartial: Bag., p. 490 "The king is the lake." - Mal. 1411 "He likes to dwell in the sovereign's land / but he does not obey the sovereign's law." - In my opinion these are sayings of law-abiding citizens about one of their number who is not too concerned with obeying the chief's will. Perhaps this is a sign of envy; hence one takes cover behind the chief's authority.

The chief causes *fear and shame*, as we find in two Malagasy proverbs: Mal. 1400 is no court wisdom, but the reaction of the ordinary people concerned: "A fierce sovereign makes afraid / a gentle sovereign makes ashamed." - Those who are afraid and ashamed are ordinary people and no courtiers. Hence ordinary people are also the speakers in this case. This sheds some interesting light on Prov. 16.14,15. - Mal. 1534 "The great (people) are like stones (carried) on the head / they both make afraid and make ashamed."

The Ewe and the Hausa mention the *different roles* of chief and people: Ewe 79 "The eyes see things / but eat them not." - The Hausa, too, know that chief and people can only act together: Hausa 101 "The head does not go on and leave the neck behind / nor the neck the head." - In this proverb the body represents the tribe (cf. I Cor 12.12ff).

(21) E.J. and J.D. Krige, *The Realm of a Rain-Queen* (London, 1943) (= Lov.).
(22) Tom Brown, *Among the Bantu Nomads* (London, 1926), p. 197ff. (= Bech.).

Besides these groups there are large numbers of individual sayings sympathetic to the chief: Mal. 1405 "The sovereign's word comes not timidly but boldly." - This refers to the public appearances of the chief and the impression he makes on the people. - Ton. 249 "The dung beetles roll a ball of dung up the hills." (= "If you see important people going to the chief, they are bringing important matters for him to deal with.") - The speakers, of course, are not themselves important, but ordinary people who observe the whole business from a distance.

The Lovedu represent their queen as very peaceloving: Lov., p. 284 "The queen does not fight." (= "Her foreign policy is appeasement.") Among the Kamba[23] the small people are warned to be cautious: Kam. 26 "A big goat does not snort without any reason." (= "A man of importance always means what he says.")

Summarizing I/3 we may observe that the proverbs sympathetic to the chief deal with six subjects from the viewpoint of the commoner: The theme 'two masters' and the people's conflict of loyalties frequently occurs. The same applies to the chief's function of order, his glory, and his mediation of blessing. His justice is mentioned as well as the fear and shame which he can cause. The division of roles between chief and people forms the subject of two proverbs.

(4) *Unclear proverbs*

The following group of six sayings is as sympathetic to the chief as I/3, but it cannot be attributed to ordinary people with the same degree of certainty. Nevertheless, some arguments in favour of popular origin can be advanced.

Mal. 686 "Don't sit still like a stone / the big not speaking / and the little having no advisers" ("big = ruler; little = people"). - The background is clear: The chief is asked to break his silence, so that the people do not remain without a leader. But by whom? One could think of a counselor, but equally of a wise man from the people. Similar advice is in fact given by the wise woman from Tekoa in II Sam. 14. - Mal. 761 "The big ones are coming / because the little ones go before." (= "In a procession those inferior in rank precede the others.") The speaker cannot be unambiguously identified, but popular origin is possible.

Mal. 1415 "It is wrong for a subject to go before a prince." - If this saying is similar to the German "Gehe nie zu deinem Fürst / wenn du nicht gerufen wirst" - which is not quite clear in the English translation -, then we could think of the advice of ordinary people to their fellows. - Ton. 32 "A chief

(23) G. Lindblom, *Kamba Folklore III* (Uppsala, 1934), p. 28ff. (= Kam.).

reigns over hyenas and crocodiles / as well as over useful animals." (= "A chief has troublesome as well as peaceful subjects.") - This, too, could be popular wisdom. - Ton. 263 "From a mother's womb cannot come two chiefs." (= "Even if they are twins, the one will be senior to the other.") Somewhat trivial popular wisdom? Fante, p. 518 "When the chief has good advisers / he reigns peacefully." - It is possible that advisers of the chief would have coined this saying. This, however, would make it unique in Africa. As it is not difficult for an ordinary tribesman to make such an observation, it might be better to think of little people (against the trend of Old Testament scholarship!).

Summary of I/4: In more than a hundred cases of African proverbs dealing with the king/ruler/chief and his court it can be proved, either with absolute or at least with relative certainty, that they have been coined by ordinary people. Six cases are unclear. But even here we find no reasons excluding popular origin.

There are, however, a number of reasons for attributing popular origin even to those sayings:

1. The claim of any other than popular origin for African proverbs would be purely speculative. There is no evidence.

2. Therefore, the methodological principle applies that among all peoples popular origin of proverbs has to be assumed until there is proof to the contrary (against Hermisson).

3. There is no civil service in Africa which could be regarded as comparable to that of Egypt, Mesopotamia or even Israel and which could function as a carrier of such wisdom. The African chief surrounds himself simply with a few wise men from his tribe.

4. Our group of 13 proverbs directed against such advisers of the chief provides a further argument against the assumption that these people have produced African proverbs.

We are, therefore, entitled, with a degree varying from great to absolute certainty, to attribute popular origin not only to the proverbs critical of the chief and court, but also to those which are sympathetic to both institutions. They have been produced by ordinary people and not by courtiers.

Thus we hope to have shown in Part I by using African parallels:

1. that there are proverbs which, though dealing with the king/ruler/ chief and his court, have nevertheless been coined by people who are themselves not members of this court.

2. In addition to this, we have found in many cases a democratic criticism of the king and his civil servants or of the chief and his counselors

respectively.

3. Thus we have already proved wrong the assumption, made by many Old Testament scholars, that the mere mention of the king or the court can be regarded as evidence for the court origin of a proverb.

4. We now have to ask ourselves, concerning the oldest Old Testament collections in Prov. 10 - 29: Is it still possible to recognize the perspective from which the royal and court sayings derive? Is this insider knowledge of courtiers or are the speakers people who are themselves distant from the court, viz. ordinary people?

(II) *The Old Testament Collections Prov. 10 - 29*

(1) Collection A (Prov. 10 - 15)

According to U. Skladny,[24] 1.1 % of the sayings of this collection deal with the king: Prov. 14.28+35. In 14.28 the people are the speakers: "In a multitude of people / is the glory of the king / but without people / a prince is ruined." - Cf. Ton. 246 "The centipede's legs are strengthened by a hundred rings." - Both proverbs are critical of the king and emphasize his dependence on the people.

14.35 "A servant who deals wisely has the king's favour / but his wrath falls on one who acts shamefully." - It is quite possible for an ordinary person to have had this experience. The *'aebaed* is not necessarily a government minister.[25]

Collection A contains a further saying for which court origin could be claimed: 11.14 "Where there is no guidance / a people falls / but in an abundance of counselors / there is safety." - But, according to McKane (ad loc.), this proverb cannot be confined to the court. It applies to all areas of life: the family, clan, tribe, and work. Ordinary people are the speakers. King and courtiers are not mentioned, as they are in the comparable Fante proverb (p. 518): "When the chief has good advisers / he reigns peacefully." - But even there court origin cannot be proved.

So, even the royal sayings fit the picture which Skladny draws of this collection in general: "Collection A presupposes the life of an agrarian

(24) Die *ältesten Spruchsammlungen in Israel* (Göttingen, 1962), p. 14
(25) W. McKane, *Proverbs* (London, 1970), ad loc.

people, as is shown by the marked appreciation of agriculture (10.5; 12.11a; 13.23a) and cattle-breeding (12.10a; 14.4)" (p.17). We may therefore conclude that Collection A contains no hard and fast evidence for the court origin of the royal sayings. On the contrary, they reflect the perspective of ordinary people.

(2) Collection B (Prov. 16 - 22.16)

16.10 "Inspired decisions are on the lips of a king / his mouth does not sin in judgment." - Cf. Bag., p. 490 "The king is the lake" (= impartial); and more generally Bech., p. 202 "God is (generally) on the side of the chief." - Both African proverbs represent experiences of little people. We may therefore have to assume the same for Prov 16.10, as the wise woman of Tekoa makes a similar pronouncement in II Sam. 14.20.[26]

16.12 "It is an abomination to kings to do evil / for the throne is established by righteousness." - I cannot understand why McKane (ad loc.) wants to confine the doing of evil to the king's subjects. The African parallels show quite clearly the insoluble connection between the king's righteousness and that of the people: Ton. 261 "When the chief limps / all his subjects limp also." (= "If a chief or leader is not honest, those who follow him will not be honest either.") - Ton. 262 "If the leader does not walk straight / those who follow him will do the same." - Mal. 1409 "A word (well) discussed makes the sovereign powerful" (= "affermit l'autorité du souverain"). - Mal. 1638/39 "If the headmen are foolish (wise) / the people are also foolish (wise)." - The establishment of the throne by righteousness is discussed in many African popular proverbs. This points to the same origin for 16.12.

16.13 "Righteous lips are the delight of a king / and he loves him who speaks what is right." - This, too, is the experience of little people dealing with "those up there".[27] Cf. Ton. 72 "You cannot dig up the hole of the ant-eater / but you may peep into it." (= "The chief cannot be forced to do anything, but you may question him without causing offence.")

16.14 "A king's wrath is a messenger of death / and a wise man will appease it." - 16.15 "In the light of the king's face / there is life / and his favour / is like the clouds that bring the spring rain." - In both cases one could

(26) Cf. H. Cazelles, *VT* 8 (1958), p. 324,

(27) So also McKane (ad loc.): "There is no reason to suppose that v.13 has in mind particularly the quality of advice tendered to the king by his inner circle of advisers, his cabinet of *sarim* or *yo'asim* ... It is rather a general statement that a community thrives on candour and that a king loves the candid man wherever he is to be found among his subjects."

be tempted to regard these proverbs as advice for courtiers (so McKane ad loc.). However, the African parallels show that these can be the experiences of ordinary people, too: Mal. 1400 "A fierce sovereign makes afraid / a gentle sovereign makes ashamed." Mal. 1534 "The great (people) are like stones (carried) on the head / they both make afraid and make ashamed."

19.10 "It is not fitting for a fool to live in luxury / much less for a slave to rule over princes." - The people obviously know their own role. Cf. Lov. p. 287 "Robes may be passed on (to strangers) / never royal rank."[28]

19.12 "A king's wrath is like the growling of a lion / but his favour is like the dew upon the grass." - Cf. my comments on 16.14,15.

20.2 "The dread wrath of a king is like the growling of a lion / he who provokes him to anger forfeits his life." - This is the experience of small people. Cf. Ton. 130 "Do not open the mouth of the roaring bull." (= "Do not speak with the angry chief.")

20.8 "A king who sits on the throne of judgment / winnows all evil with his eyes." - Cf. 16.10 (Bech. p. 202, and Bag. p. 490) and Mal. 1411 "He likes to dwell in the sovereign's land / but he does not obey the sovereign's law." - Fante, p. 518 "A snare is destroyed / when an elephant places his foot in it." - The Fante know of no appeal against the chief's decision: "After the elephant (= chief) there is no other animal." - All these proverbs are of popular origin. The same applies to 20.26: "A wise king winnows the wicked / and drives the wheel over them."

20.18 "Plans are established by counsel / by wise guidance wage war." - This proverb critical of king and court is a warning of the people to "those up there". Cf. Mal. 1409 "A word (well) discussed makes the sovereign powerful"; also 11.14; 15.22 and Fante, p. 518 "If Otsibo says he can do something / he does it with his followers." 20.28 "Loyalty and faithfulness (*haesaed wae'aemaet*) preserve the king / and his throne is upheld by righteousness (*haesaed*). - This saying is a warning to the king by the people, as the parallels show: Aki., p. 224 "A potent man does not insult two seasons" (without being removed). Ton. 4 "The elephant is the trunk." - Without his subjects the chief can do nothing. Ton. 260 "Take care of it / it will take care of you." (= "Take care of your people, and they will take care of you.") Ton. 269 "People are wealth" (= " ... are the basis of your power"). Also Fante, p. 518 "Though the elephant is huge / his domain is looked after by the duiker." 21.1 "The king's heart is a stream of water in the hand of

---

(28) The situation described is regarded as contrary to the divine order (so also H. Ringgren, *Sprüche* [Göttingen, 3rd ed. 1980], ad loc.). On the formal structure: x is not the case / the less y cf. McKane, ad loc.).

Yahweh / he turns it wherever he will." - McKane (ad loc.) regards this proverb as critical of the civil service: "The king is not dependent on the experience of *sarim* or *hakamim* or *yo'asim* for guidance in state matters ... (He is) directly influenced and controlled by Yahweh." Consequently the people are the speakers and not the courtiers! 21.22 "A wise man scales the city of the mighty / and brings down the stronghold in which they trust."[29] Cf. my comments on 20.18. 21.31 "The horse is made ready for the day of battle / but the victory belongs to Yahweh." - This is probably an observation of the people like 20.18 and 21.22.

Collection B, according to Skladny, describes the "difference which still exists between the most mighty and the almighty" (p. 29). This shows the perspective of ordinary people who call upon God for protection from royal arbitrariness. The "king is no absolute ruler, he has got no ... power in his own right, but only as a delegate, a tool of Yahweh" (Skladny, ibid.). This tendency critical of the king is a sure indication of popular origin.

The economic background of Collection B - "agriculture, handicraft, and trade ... many images are taken from town life" (p. 41) - points to farmers and petty bourgeois as the creators of these sayings. Diametrically opposed to these results is then Skladny's claim that Collection B is intended for diplomats and civil servants ("Beamten- und Diplomatenspiegel", p. 46). Again a scholar's presuppositions and the coercion of the hypotheses (in this case the royal court hypothesis) have triumphed over the Old Testament facts, which the same scholar had earlier on correctly identified!

(3) Collection C (Prov. 25-27)

25.1 is the title of this collection and no proverb. 25.2 "It is the glory of God to conceal things / but the glory of kings is to search things out." - According to Skladny (p. 54), this proverb deals with the king in his function as judge. The Old Testament gives us many examples of ordinary people bringing their case before the king (II Sam. 14.1-24; I Kings 3.16-28). - Cf. Ton. 23 "It is those in front who ask about the buffalo." (= "A difficult case must be dealt with by people in authority.")

With this court-critical saying the people appeal directly to the chief. - Bag. p. 490 "The king is the lake" (impartial). - But from bad experience ordinary people sometimes advise to the contrary: Mal. 1415 "It is wrong for a subject to go before a prince" - but this proverb may not refer to legal procedure.

(29) Cf. 16.32; 24.5-6.

25.3 "As the heavens for height / and the earth for depth / so the mind of kings is unsearchable." - According to Skladny (ibid.), this proverb gives the reason for respect before the king. It is of popular origin like Bav. 19 "The pot which is poured into (the chief) / is better than that which is cooked." 25.4,5 "take away the dross from the silver / and the smith has material for a vessel / take away the wicked from the presence of the king / and his throne will be established in righteousness." - A text critical of the court. Skladny (ibid.) regards it as critical of those around the king, not of the monarch himself. This reflects the attitude of ordinary people. - Cf. Mal. 1438 "A horse of honours: dead today / it is substituted tomorrow" (= "a high officer").25.6,7 "Do not put yourself forward in the king's presence / or stand in the place of the great / for it is better to be told 'Come up here' / than to be put lower in the presence of the prince." - A popular exhortation to an ordinary person (contra Ringgren, ad loc.) to behave himself at court. He is not to stand in the place of the great, because, according to Skladny (ibid.), he is quite obviously not part of them! - Cf. Mal. 761 "The big ones are coming / because the little ones go before." - In a procession the place of ordinary people is at the beginning, that of the dignitaries at the end.

Skladny summarizes: "In Collection C the king is regarded with great respect, but from the perspective of someone who does not belong to his company" (p. 54). Consequently we are dealing with folk wisdom.

Because of its high esteem of agriculture and handicraft, Skladny (p. 56) regards Collection C as intended for farmers and craftsmen ("Bauern- und Handwerkerspiegel"). So, one might have thought that no further obstacles would stand in the way of the popular origin of C! But no! Skladny cheerfully proceeds to throw his results out of the window and put on the spectacles of the royal court hypothesis. Now the popular wisdom of Collection C appears to him as adaptation of court wisdom to the world of ordinary people (p. 57). I have already commented on Skladny's blindness elsewhere.[30]

(4) Collection D (Prov. 28 - 29)

Skladny regards D as a collection addressed to *rulers (Regentenspiegel)*. This thesis will have to be examined. If it were true, we would have to ask, whether each individual proverb had already been coined for this purpose.

28.2 "When a land transgresses / it has many rulers / but with a man of

(30) note 2, esp. p. 268-9
(31) I am deleting *yodea'* with McKane (ad loc.) as a glosse of *mebin*.

understanding[31]/ its stability will long continue." – Cf. Ton. 107 and Bantu, p. 48: "Authority (power) is the tail of the water-rat." (= "A chief's power slips away from the one who possesses it.") – Mash., p. 175 "Dew soon dries up / so will chieftaincy." – As the African parallels show, 28.2 can be understood as a proverb critical of rulers. But, as Ringgren (ad loc) rightly emphasizes, the people receive their share of the blame, too. This proverb may originate among old, but ordinary people who have seen many rulers and many uprisings. 28.3 "A 'wicked'[32] man who oppresses the poor / is a beating rain that leaves no food". – This is the picturesque language of the *dallim* (poor). – Cf. Ton. 44 "Do not whirl a snake in the air / when you have killed it / the ones which remain in their holes / see you." – Both cases represent a clear warning of the poor to their oppressors.

28.15 "A roaring lion or a charging bear (what is it?) / (answer:) a wicked ruler over a poor people." – As farmers and cattle-breeders are often attacked by wild beasts, it is now the king who attacks them. A sigh from the lips of the people! Cf. Mal. 1386 "Great people are open to shame / and the small are open to fear." 28.16 "A ruler who lacks understanding / is a cruel oppressor / but he who hates unjust gain / will prolong his days." – Cf. Fante, p. 518 "If you see a stick that will pierce your eye / break it off" (= "removal of a chief"). – The Old Testament saying is critical of the king and, like the Fante proverb, to be attributed to the people. 29.2 When the righteous are in authority / the people rejoice / but when the wicked rule / the people groan." – Cf. Ton. 255 "Authority has no sweetness". – A typical complaint of the poor man about the king.

29.4 "By justice a king gives stability to the land / but one who exacts 'gifts' ruins it." – A deeply felt sigh of the ordinary people, perhaps against Solomon's taxation? – On the oppression of the poor cf. here also Ton. 255. The chief's financial dealings are described by Mal. 1418 "Like demanding payment of debt from a prince / it is the creditor that does the coaxing."

29.12 "If a ruler listens to falsehood / all his officials will be wicked." – Ton. 261 "When the chief limps / all his subjects limp also." (= "If the chief or leader is not honest, those who follow him will not be honest either.") – Similarly Ton. 262 "If the leader does not walk straight / those who follow him will do the same." – All three are popular proverbs. 29.14 "If a king judges the poor with equity / his throne will be established for ever." – The Chagga, too, know the chief as helper in need: Chag. 17a "If the cattle are finished / yet have we a Chief." – In both cases poor people are the speakers. 29.26 "Many seek the favour of a ruler / but from Yahweh a man gets

(32) I am reading *rasa'* with LXX against the MT's *ras*. McKane (ad loc.) suggests *ros* (= *ro's*).

justice." - A popular saying critical of the king, which plays Yahweh off against the ruler.

In Collection D, too, we find royal and court sayings coined by ordinary people. These are (contra Skladny, p. 58) precisely statements about the king, and not directly addressed to him. This does not exclude them from secondary usage in a Regentenspiegel, but this type of wisdom originates among the people, and not at court.

Comparing D to the Regentenspiegel II Sam. 23.1-7, Skladny finds "agreement in essential points" (p. 67). On closer examination these can be reduced to the luck of the just ruler (vv. 3-5) and to an exhortation to eliminate the worthless *beliyya'al* (vv. 6+7). In both cases it is therefore more than doubtful whether we are dealing with a Regentenspiegel at all. If this were so in the case of D (in spite of Prov. 29.26), we should have to regard this as secondary usage of original folk wisdom. It seems to me more appropriate to regard D as a collection of sayings about the righteous man. The king is precisely no independent subject in D, but simply a special case of how to act justly, and therefore D cannot be a Regentenspiegel.

In the case of the African proverbs, as I hope to have shown, popular origin is either highly probable or virtually certain. Now Prov. 10 - 29 show a similar picture: There is not one single royal or court saying, where popular origin is excluded. When the sayings are critical of the court or king, popular origin is very probable. The African parallels suggest to me that it is much more likely that the royal and court sayings in Prov. 10 - 29 originated among ordinary people rather than at court, because their perspective is that of the commoner and not that of the courtier.

In A the royal sayings have been placed within the framework of a collection for farmers and in B within one for farmers and petty bourgeois (contra Skladny). In C they appear in a collection for farmers and craftsmen, which, however, is popular and no court wisdom (contra Skladny). While in A - C the framework of popular wisdom is easily recognized, matters are more complicated in D. The Regentenspiegel claimed by Skladny cannot be proved, because, first, it is not the king who is addressed and, second, he is not the main subject either. D contains sayings about the just man, and in this context mention is also made of the just dealings of a king. The royal sayings in D consist of popular wisdom, but the collection as such may well have been published by the "men of Hezekiah", like Collection C. We may therefore conclude that the origin of wisdom at the royal court, claimed or just repeated by so many scholars, cannot be proved from the royal and court sayings in Prov. 10 - 29. The great majority of these sayings rather supports the common sense argument for the popular origin of proverbs.

What then is the theological significance of the problem of the origin of Israelite wisdom? For an answer, we have to bear in mind that we now encounter Prov. as part of the canon of the Hebrew Bible. This poses an ecclesiological problem, both for Judaism and Christianity: Does Proverbs represent only the experiences of an intellectual elite, or does the book also voice the experiences of God and life found among very ordinary people? Have contributions from the latter layer of society also found their way into the canon of the Hebrew Bible, if only - but possibly deliberately - under the protection of Solomonic pseudonymity?

It is these ordinary people who form an ever decreasing proportion of the membership of West European churches. Thus Erhard S. Gerstenberger, at the IOSOT congress in Salamanca, has drawn the following conclusion: "The creative reality, in which each exegete finds himself, is reflected by his research. European Old Testament scholars reproduce, according to their various traditions, a deeply rooted imperialism, a predominant individualism, and a comforting spirituality. Some Latin American exegetes, on the other hand, deliberately start from the situation of the poor and exploited majority of the population."[33] While the customary rejoinder in Europe has been that the Latin Americans read their own revolutionary theology into the Old Testament, one does not notice the beam in one's own eye!

This beam has now been clearly uncovered by another Wolff pupil, Frank Crüsemann (note 4, p. 1-17). He proves that Wellhausen's and Budde's glorification of the Israelite monarchy is directly derived from their german-nationalist political convictions (Israelite king = German emperor; the monarchy = order; the period of the judges = chaos). However, since Max Weber and Martin Noth a much more positive view of the period of the Judges has appeared in our research into the Historical books. In Wisdom research, by contrast, the glorification of the king as the guarantor of order remains unbroken.

The question of the origin of Israelite wisdom therefore takes on an ecclesiological as well as a political dimension. There is a danger that one might now fall into the other extreme. My own recipe for the avoidance of such pitfalls is, if not very original, at least simple: Scholars should stick strictly to the facts mentioned in the Old Testament and be very wary of ideologically based hypotheses, such as 'royal court', 'schools', and 'a professional class of wise men'.

(33) E.S. Gerstenberger, "Der Realitätsbezug alttestamentlicher Exegese", *SVT* 36 (1984), p. 132-44.

3

The Leopard's Spots
Biblical and African Wisdom in Proverbs

I dedicate this paper to my Heidelberg teacher, Professor Claus Westermann, on the occasion of his 80th birthday on 7th October 1989.[1] His essay in the field of Wisdom, "Weisheit im Sprichwort",[2] was probably the most important contribution since G. von Rad's book 'Wisdom in Israel'.[3]

Von Rad[4] describes the history of research into Wisdom in three phases: (I) First of all, Wisdom was regarded as a product of the Second Temple congregation (I mention only the so-called 'dogma of retribution'), then there followed (II) the so-called 'Egyptian' phase in which one derived Israel's Wisdom from that of her oriental neighbours. But, according to von Rad, "there is every appearance that the process of comparison with the wisdom of neighbouring cultures has more or less petered out",[5] and he therefore makes a determined plea for entering phase III, namely the investigation of the specific characteristics of Israelite Wisdom.

And this is precisely Westermann's starting-point: (I) A proverb has to be explained *primarily* from the situation in which it arises and only *secondarily* against the background of the collections. (II) The proverb genre is to be found among *illiterate* peoples. (III) *All* Wisdom is originally expressed in proverbs; no other forms of expression are extant yet. (IV) In the Old Testament and other sophisticated civilizations we encounter a late stage of

(1) It appeared as part of the Festschrift, *Schöpfung und Befreiung*, ed.s R.Albertz, F.W.Golka, J.Kegler (Stuttgart, 1989), pp. 149-65.
(2) published in 1971, reprinted in 1974 in *Forschung am Alten Testament II* (München), pp. 149-61. Since then Westermann has set out his thesis in detail in *Wurzeln der Weisheit. Die ältesten Sprüche Israels und anderer Völker* (Göttingen, 1990).
(3) G. von Rad, *Weisheit in Israel* (Neukirchen-Vluyn, 1970).
(4) *Weisheit in Israel*, p.20ff.
(5) *Weisheit in Israel*, p.22

the proverb genre which has its actual life in 'primitive' cultures. (V) The validity of these theses would have to be proved from a representative 'overview' of the proverbs of 'primitive' cultures.[6]

But in his essay Westermann is not yet in a position to provide such an overview, but can only hint at it with examples from a collection of the proverbs of the Ho tribe.[7] The present author has therefore undertaken a somewhat sketchy comparison between biblical and African proverbs.[8] It is intended as an 80th birthday present for Claus Westermann, but also commemorates his father, Diedrich Westermann, the famous Berlin Africanist.

In his course of lectures, entitled "Job and Wisdom", given in Heidelberg during the summer semester 1975, Westermann divided the biblical proverbs into seven main areas: (I) Man, (II) Man in Society, (III) Work and Possessions, (IV) Public Life, (V) Wisdom and Folly, (VI) God and Man, (VII) The Righteous and the Wicked. The first three and the last two groups he divided further into subsections. The present author makes use of Westermann's division in comparing biblical with African proverbs, with the former being taken from the oldest collections in Prov. 10-29. I am hoping to be able to show on the one hand that the aspects of life covered by the biblical and African proverbs are very much the same, but that on the other hand the theological Wisdom of Israel goes far beyond the folk wisdom of Africa.

I   Man

Westermann subdivides as follows: (1) Observations of human nature, (2) Observations using comparisons, (3) Joy and grief, (4) Speech and silence, (5) Human actions. (2) and (4) are most common in Prov. 10-29, in Africa all five subgroups occur frequently.

(6) Cf. for this summary my chapter on 'Wisdom schools', pp.4-15.
(7) Jakob Spieth, *Die Ewe-Stämme*, 1906, pp. 599-612.
(8) Ruth Finnegan refutes the assumption of many Old Testament scholars that the art form of the Book of Proverbs does not bear comparison with the proverbs of Africa: "It is clear that some sort of heightened speech, in one form or another, is commonly used in proverbs: *...this serves to set them apart from ordinary speech*" (Ruth Finnegan, *Oral Literature in Africa*, Oxford 1970, p. 403). Even the *parallelismus membrorum* can frequently be found.

(1) Observations of human nature

Prov. 14.30 A tranquil mind gives life to the flesh / but passion makes the bones rot.

Prov. 17.19 He who loves transgression loves strife / he who makes his door high seeks destruction.

Prov. 18.12 Before destruction a man's heart is haughty / but humility goes before honour.

Bantu[9] p.46 An elephant does not die of one (broken) rib (= A strong man does not lose heart through a single misfortune).

Bav.[10] 29 A dirty person does not see himself.

Lov.[11] p.291 Man is an elephant / he does not eat one kind of plant only (= versatility).

Bech.[12] p.202 He has many eyes (= is easily attracted by everything in turn).

(2) Observations using comparisons

Prov. 12.14 From the fruit of his words a man is satisfied with good / and the work of a man's hand comes back to him.

Prov. 14.17 A man of quick temper acts foolishly / but a 'plotter' is hated.

Prov. 20.5 The purpose in a man's mind is like deep water / but a man of understanding will draw it out.

Masai[13] 13 He separates himself from his friends like a sick donkey (lone-wolf).

Aki.[14] p.214 A white dog does not bite another white dog.

Masai 51 Baboons do not go far from the place of their birth (= similarly with people).

Nandi[15] 14 They are alike: raider and home-stayer (= similar risk).

Hausa[16] 70 Man is like a pepper / till you have chewed it / you do not know how hot it is.

(9) H.P.Junod, *Bantu Heritage*, Johannesburg 1938, p.46ff (= Bantu). The explanations of the original collectors and editors are given in brackets (= ...).

(10) H.A.Stayt, *The Bavenda*, London 1931, 360-61 (= Bav.).

(11) E.J. and J.D.Krige, *The Realm of a Rain-Queen*, London 1943 (= Lov.).

(12) Tom Brown, *Among the Bantu Nomads*, London 1926, p. 197ff (= Bech.).

(13) A.C.Hollis, *The Masai. Their Language and Folklore*, Oxford 1905 (= Masai).

(14) C.Cagnolo, *The Akikuyu. Their Customs, Traditions and Folklore*, Nyeri/Kenya 1933, p. 214ff (= Aki.).

(15) A.C.Hollis, *The Nandi. Their Language and Folklore*, Oxford 1969 = 1909 (= Nandi).

(16) R.S.Rattray, *Hausa-Folklore II*, Oxford 1913, p.254ff (= Hausa).

(3) Joy and grief

Prov. 14.10   The heart knows its own bitterness / and no stranger shares its joy.

Prov. 13.13   Even in laughter the heart is sad / and the end of joy is grief.

Prov. 15.13   A glad heart makes a cheerful countenance / but by sorrow of heart the spirit is broken.

Mal.[17] 2136   Don't be sorry that you have missed the funeral / for there will be many more taken ill.

Mal. 1007   In great trouble: go up (the river) / he is eaten by the crocodile / go down (the river) / he is eaten by the alligator.

Mal. 1027   The sorrow I can bear / but not the professional mourner.

Mal. 1145   The sweet is in the bitter.

(4) Speech and silence

Prov. 10.18   He who conceals hatred has lying lips / and he who utters slander is a fool.

Prov. 10.19   When words are many, transgression is not lacking / but he who restrains his lips is prudent.

Prov. 18.21   Death and life are in the power of the tongue / and those who love it will eat its fruits.

Mal. 491   The word invites you to stay the night / but the countenance sends you home again the same day.

Mal. 554   Good words are food / bad words poison.

Mal. 567   Scandal is like an egg / when it is hatched, it has wings.

Mal. 568   Don't speak evil of people before their friends.

Many African societies do not only use proverbs in order to convince someone, but also for the purpose of embellishing speeches. "It is part of the art of an accomplished orator to adorn his rhetoric with apt and appealing proverbs."[18]

(5) Human actions

Prov. 17.13   If a man returns evil for good / evil will not depart from his house.

Prov. 19.16   He who keeps the commandment keeps his life / he who despises the word will die.

(17) J.A.Houlder, *OHABOLANA or Malagassy proverbs I&II*, Antananarivo 1915/16; French translations by H. Noyer (= Mal.).

(18) Finnegan, *Oral Literature*, 415

Prov. 21.14   A gift in secret averts anger / and a bribe in the bosom, strong wrath.

Fante[19] p.519   The hen's feet do not kill her chicks.

Fante p.523   The crab does not give birth to a bird.

Kaf.[20] p.181   *Bakuba* is far away / no person has ever reached it (= Be content!).

Chag.[21] 3   The dead gazelle teaches the live gazelle (= German proverb: Durch Erfahrung wird man klug).

II   Man in Society

Westermann divides this section into seven subgroups: (1) Husband and wife, (2) Parents and children, (3) Old and young, (4) The friend, (5) The slave (servant), (6) Eating and drinking, (7) Education. This last group is the most important in the Bible, whereas all of them occur frequently in Africa.

(1)   Husband and wife

Prov. 11.16   A gracious woman gets honour / and 'active'[22] men get riches.

Prov. 11.22   Like a gold ring in a swine's snout / is a beautiful woman without discretion.

Prov. 21.9   It is better to live in a corner of the housetop / than in a house shared with a contentious woman.

Fante p.524   A wife is like a blanket / for even though it scratches you / you are cold without it.

Fante p.524   Do not tell your wife anything that cannot be said in public.

Bantu p.50   To marry is to put a snake in one's handbag.

Hausa 125   It is not the act of marrying that is difficult / it is getting the money (to marry).

(19) J.B.Christensen, "The Role of Proverbs in Fante Culture", in E.P.Skinner (ed.), *Peoples and Cultures of Africa*, New York 1973, p. 509ff (= Fante).

(20) G.McCall, *Kaffir Folk-lore*, 1892 (= Kaf.).

(21) C.Dundas, *Kilimanjaro and its People*, London 1924, p.341ff (= Chag.).

(22) O.Plöger, *Sprüche Salomos (Proverbia)*, BK XVII, Neukirchen-Vluyn 1984, ad.loc.: "...und Tatkräftige gewinnen Reichtum".

(2) Parents and children

Prov. 15.20	A wise son makes a glad father / but a foolish man despises his mother.
Prov. 17.6	Grandchildren are the crown of the aged / and the glory of sons is their fathers.
Prov. 17.21	A stupid son is a grief to a father / and the father of a fool has no joy.
Aki. p.215	A son is like his father.
Aki. p.222	A son for whom his father works the field / does not know that things are precious.
Bech. p.200	Happy is she who has born a daughter / a boy is the son of his mother-in-law.
Mal. 1743	Equals are husband and wife / the little and the big are parent and child.

(3) Old and young

This is not a frequent subject in Prov., but rather more so in Africa:

Prov. 16.31	A hoary head is a crown of glory / it is gained in a righteous life.
Prov. 20.29	The glory of young men is their strength / but the beauty of old men is their grey hair.
Fante p.516	The child bows to the elders.
Bantu p.47	A hare gave orders to an elephant (= A child gave orders to a grown-up person).
Ewe[23] 119	Respect the elders / they are your fathers.
Lov. p.105	The stick even of a child / helps the adult across.
Bech. p.200	The young bird does not crow / until it hears the old ones.

(4) The friend

Prov. 17.17	A friend loves at all times / and a brother is born for adversity.
Prov. 18.24	There are friends who pretend to be friends[24] / but there is a friend who sticks closer than a brother.
Prov. 27.10	consists of three proverbs: Your friend, and your father's friend, do not forsake. Do not go to your brother's house in the day of your calamity.

(23) A.B.Ellis, *The EWE-Speaking Peoples*, London 1890 (= Ewe).

Better is a neighbour who is near than a brother who is far away.

Bantu p.53   It is a second marriage (= new friends).

Mash.[25] p.174   One thumb will not kill a louse (= A man without friends is powerless).

Bag.[26] p.491   I had a number of friends / before calamity befell me.

Aki. p.224   Hearts do not meet another like roads.

Hausa 103   A ladder above a ladder / a friend's friend.

(5) The slave / servant

Prov. 17.2   A slave who deals wisely will rule over a son who acts shamefully / and will share the inheritance as one of the brothers.

Prov. 19.10   It is not fitting for a fool to live in luxury / much less for a slave to rule over princes.

Prov. 29.19   By mere words a servant is not disciplined / for though he understands, he will not give heed.

Hausa 129   A slave does not make himself equal of a free man.

Hausa 130   The slave of Maku is one with Maku.

Mal. 1538   The old slave took another wife / he became three before his price went down.

Mal. 1552   A slave sat down in a warm place / he finds it hard to move.

(6) Eating and drinking

While there are only three occurrences in Prov. 10-29, Africa has much more material:

Prov. 11.26   The people curse him who holds back grain / but a blessing is on the head of him who sells it.

Prov. 13.23   The fallow ground of the poor yields much food / but it is swept away through injustice.

Prov. 15.17   Better a dinner of herbs with love in it / than a fatted ox and hatred with it.

Mal. 615   A big pot that has cooked meat has always some morsels left in it.

---

(24) Plöger, BK, ad.loc.: "Es gibt Freunde, die sich gegenseitig Böses antun /....

(25) C.Bullock, *The Mashona. The Indigenous Natives of S. Rhodesia*, Cape Town and Johannesburg 1927 (= Mash.).

(26) John Roscoe, *The Baganda*, London 1911 (= Bag.).

Mal. 620   When I am going to eat, call a few /
           but when I am going to work, fetch many.
Mal. 400   It was not the rice's fault to boil over /
           but the cook is in a temper.
Mal. 600   A labourer does not fill his belly (= his own disadvantage).

(7) Education
   In Prov. 10-29 this is the only large group from section II:
   Prov. 10.17 He who heeds instruction is on the path to life /
                but he who rejects reproof goes astray.
   Prov. 12.1   Whoever loves discipline loves knowlege /
                but he who hates reproof is stupid.
   Prov. 13.24 He who spares the rod hates his son /
                but he who loves him is diligent to discipline him.
   Fante p.518 A child is talked to in proverbs.
   Fante p.519 One does not send a child on an errand /
                then look to see whether or not he is pleased.
   Bav. 32   A child forbidden an axe /
                leaves a knife of its own accord.
   Lov. p.122   I told you, O novice /
                but you plugged your ears with plugs of wood.

It is said of the Chaga that they have four kinds of possessions: land, cattle, water, and proverbs.[27] According to Ruth Finnegan, in illiterate societies proverbs provide a tool for education and for transmitting cultural traditions. "Proverbs with their implicit generalized import are clearly a suitable and succinct form in which to verbalize socially prescribed actions and attitudes."[28]

But proverbs have not been coined for the purpose of education, as some Old Testament scholars assume. "... proverbs are in practice cited in a whole variety of situations, and only in some of them does there seem to be any intentionally educational purpose."[29]

(27) O.F.Raum, *Chaga Childhood*, London 1940, p.217.
(28) Finnegan, *Oral Literature*, p.413.
(29) ibid.

III Work and Possessions

Westermann divides this section into (1) The farmer, (2) The messenger, (3) The industrious man and the sluggard, (4) Poor and rich, (5) Treasures gained by wickedness do not profit, (6) Alms and charity. (3) and (4) are the largest groups.

(1) The farmer

Prov. 14.4   Where there are no oxen, there is no grain /
              but abundant crops come by the strength of the ox.
Bantu p.50   Borrowed hoe does not plough (=Do your work yourself).
Bav. 12   One finger cannot pick up stamped mealies (= work
              together!).
Lov. p.284   The one who loses the cattle /
              is the one who herds them.
Mal. 1206   Driving a hundred oxen / minding a thousand sheep/
              those that go astray / are more than those that get home.
Mal. 1212   Drive an ox with a long tail through the mud /
              and the driver gets bespattered.

It is my impression that 'the farmer' is of no special interest in Prov. 10-29. It is rather the case that images from the farmer's world are used to make statements of general significance (e.g. in 12.11). The same is true of the African examples.

(2) The messenger

In an illiterate culture the messenger is of great importance. However, in Prov. 10-29 we only find half a dozen references, and many of them can be assigned to I/4 (Speech and silence).

Prov. 13.17   A bad messenger plunges men into trouble /
              but a faithful envoy brings healing.
Prov. 25.25   Like cold water to the thirsty soul /
              so is good news from a far country.
Bech. p.201   A harbinger is the lamp of his friends.
Kam. 30[30]   One message involves another message (= the answer).
Aki. p.220   He who takes an embassy / has no concern in it.

---

(30) G.Lindblom, *Kamba Folklore III*, Uppsala 1934, p.28ff (= Kam.).

Mal. 1204 'Go far' thinks the sender /
'Don't go at all' thinks the messenger.

Ton.[31]683 The burden of the mouth is not heavy (= The oral message
entrusted to you is not a burden).

(3) The industrious man and the sluggard

Prov. 10.5 A son who gathers in the summer is prudent /
but a son who sleeps in harvest brings shame.

Prov. 13.4 The soul of the sluggard craves, and gets nothing/
while the soul of the diligent is richly supplied.

Prov. 22.13 The sluggard says, 'There is a lion outside /
I shall be slain in the streets'.

Bantu p.50 The crown of a man is (in) his hands.

Lov. p.284 The sluggard has no locusts /
even if they sleep in his courtyard.

Kaf. p.181 One fly does not provide for another (= A saying of the
industrious to the idle, meaning that each should work for
himself as the flies do).

Hausa 55 Till he dies he will not even twist a *kaba* palm-leaf (= Good
for nothing).

Mal. 672 If you will neither milk the cow nor hold the calf /
you ought not to skim off the cream.

(4) Poor and rich

Prov. 10.15 The rich man's wealth is his strong city /
the poverty of the poor is their ruin.[32]

Prov. 11.4 Riches do not profit in the day of wrath /
but righteousness delivers from death.

Prov. 14.20 The poor is disliked even by his neighbour /
but the rich man has many friends.

Fante p.513 A good name cannot be eaten /
it is money that counts.

Bantu p.49 Wealth is dew (= It melts like dew in the sun).

Kaf. p.190 You drink out of an old cup (= inherited wealth).

Aki. p.215 He who has had his fill becomes thoughtless.

---

(31) H.P.Junod and A.A.Jaques, *The Wisdom of the Tonga-Shangaan People*, Cleveland,
Transvaal 1936 (= Ton.).

(32) Cf. Plöger, BK, ad.loc.

(5) Treasures gained by wickedness do not profit

Prov. 10.2   Treasures gained by wickedness do not profit /
              but righteousness delivers from death.

Prov. 11.1   A false balance is an abomination to the LORD /
              but just weight is his delight.

Prov. 15.27   He who is greedy for unjust gain makes trouble for his
              household / but he who hates bribes will live.

Aki. p.214   Virtue is better than wealth.

Bag. p.491   Risk is never absent from those who seek wealth.

Mal. 736   Love of money is the tail of witchcraft.

Mal. 778   Got wrongly and spent foolishly.

(6) Alms and charity

Prov. 11.25   A liberal man will be enriched /
              and one who waters himself will be watered.

Prov. 14.21   He who despises his neighbour is a sinner /
              but happy is he who is kind to the poor.

Prov. 19.17   He who is kind to the poor lends to the LORD /
              and he will repay him for his deed.

Mal. 735   Man is the receiver / but riches the giver of blessings.

Mal. 774   Spilt grain of rice are friends of the fowls.

Aki. p.224   Many friends empty the pocket.

Mas.[33] p.220 Many people are good / if we want to have something
              (from them).

Hausa 18   They pat the cow / before they begin to milk her.

Summarizing section III we may conclude that groups (3) and (4), the industrious man/the sluggard and poor/rich, are the most common in Prov. 10-29. (5) and (6) Treasures gained by wickedness and alms and charity are also important groups. The fact that (2) 'the messenger' occurs only half a dozen times is explained by the overlap with I/4 'Speech and silence'. The farmer (1) represents no independent group.

---

(33) M.Merker, *Die Masai*, 1904 (= Mas.).

IV   Public Life

Westermann provides no further subdivisions for this section. It includes the royal and court sayings which have been coined from the perspective of ordinary people.[34]

Prov. 11.14   Where there is no guidance, a people falls /
              but in an abundance of counsellors there is safety.

Prov. 14.35   A servant who deals wisely has the king's favour/
              but his wrath falls on one who acts shamefully.

Prov. 18.5   It is not good to be partial to a wicked man /
              or to deprive a righteous man of justice.

Prov. 18.18   The lot puts an end to disputes /
              and decides between powerful contenders.

Fante p.518   One cannot make the same tracks as an elephant
              (= chief).

ibid.   When the chief has good advisers /
              he reigns peacefully (cf. Prov. 11.14).

Bantu p.47   Two lions fear each other (=Two chiefs show respect
              to each other).

Lunda[35] p.282 The talking bird was master / he scattered his
              following (= A headman ... who nags will soon find
              himself alone).

Kam. 26   A big goat does not snort without any reason
              (= A man of importance always means what he says).

There are about three dozen occurrences of this subject in Prov. 10-29.[36] Particularly noteworthy is the small thematic collection in 16.10-15.

---

(34) Cf. "The Royal and Court Sayings and the Origin of Israelite Wisdom", pp.16-35.
(35) F.H.Melland, *In Witch-bound Africa*, London 1923 (= Lunda).
(36) For further African examples cf. "The Royal and Court Sayings", pp.16-35.

V   Wisdom and Folly

For this section, too, Westermann gives no further subdivisions.

Prov. 10.14 Wise men lay up knowledge /
             but the babbling of a fool brings ruin near.
Prov. 12.11 He who tills his land will have plenty of bread /
             but he who follows worthless pursuits has no sense.
Prov. 13.14 The teaching of the wise is a fountain of life /
             that one may avoid the snares of death.

This statement already shows a high degree of reflection. It is hardly a folk proverb.

Prov. 16.16 To get wisdom is better than gold /
             to get understanding is to be chosen rather than
             silver.[37] (Cf. my comments on 13.14).

We should also mention the most commonly quoted *proverb pair*.[38]

Prov. 26.4+5 Answer not a fool according to his folly /
              lest you be like him yourself.
              Answer a fool according to his folly /
              lest he be wise in his own eyes.
Bantu p.51   The wise man examines the thoughts of other people.
ibid   Wisdom is found on the way (= A man becomes wise
              when he travels).
Kaonde[39] p.281 Follow as a bitch follows / not as a dog
                  (= A woman is wiser than a man).
Bag. p.490   Sense has left you like a person who nods in sleep /
              before he has spread his mat to sleep upon.
Masai 29   We begin by being foolish /
              and we become wise by experience.

A beautiful description of experiential wisdom.

---

(37) Plöger, BK, ad.loc. translates: "Was ist besser als Gold? Erwerb von Weisheit / und Erwerb von Einsicht kostbarer als Silber".
(38) Cf. Ted Hildebrandt, "Compositional Units in Proverbs 10-29", *JBL* 107, 1988, pp.207-24.
(39) F.H.Melland, *In Witch-bound Africa*, 1923 (= Kaonde).

VI God and Man

Westermann subdivides as follows: (1) Worship, sacrifice, and prayer, (2) The limitations of Wisdom, (3) God sees everything, (4) The creator of humanity (there is no mention of the creator of the world), (5) God's activity in human life, (6) God remains beyond all opposites (Matthew 5.45). (3) and (5) are the strongest subgroups in Prov. 10-29.

(1) Worship, sacrifice, and prayer

Prov. 15.8	The sacrifice of the wicked is an abomination to the LORD / but the prayer of the upright is his delight.
Prov. 15.29	The LORD is far from the wicked / but he hears the prayer of the righteous.
Prov. 21.3	To do righteousness and justice / is more acceptable to the LORD than sacrifice.
Ton. 785	One cannot offer a sacrifice (to the dead) for other people.
Ton. 885	The ancestor's spirit's plate is one (for all).

(= When people meet for a sacrifice or a propiciation ceremony each one must eat from the plate consecrated to the spirit. This shows the unity of those participating in such ceremonies).

Hausa 6	Duck / you have nothing to do with the sacrifice.
Hausa 123	There is no getting a thing / if you seek it from Allah.

Apart from the sapiential polemic against sacrifice (Prov. 21.3), this can hardly be regarded as an independent group. A few proverbs, e.g. Prov. 15.8+29, also come under section VII (The Righteous and the Wicked). More than 2000 Malagassy proverbs do not mention worship, sacrifice and prayer even once, and also in 1000 Tonga proverbs this subject is only mentioned twice (in relation to the ancestral spirits). Hence we can only conclude, in spite of Leo Perdue's argument to the contrary,[40] that apart from the polemic against sacrifice proverbial wisdom was hardly concerned with worship and prayer.

---

(40) L.G.Perdue, *Wisdom and Cult*, Missoula / Mont. 1977.

(2) The limitations of Wisdom
  Prov. 10.22   The blessing of the LORD makes rich /
                and he adds no sorrow with it.
  Prov. 16.1   The plans of the mind belong to man /
                but the answer of the tongue is from the LORD.[41]
  Prov. 19.21   Many are the plans in the mind of a man /
                but it is the purpose of the LORD that will be
                established.
  The Akikuyu have a similar proverb:
  Aki. p.218   The designs of one's heart do not arrive /
                but those of God arrive.
  Ton. 837   No man can fight with heaven.
  Masai 68   He who separates the paths (= the Almighty).

Compared to the ten occurrences in Prov 10–29, the three African proverbs known to me look pitiful. This is a clear indication that 'the limitations of Wisdom' is part of theological Wisdom and hence not further developed in the folk wisdom of Africa. Here the African proverbs provide an effective control test for von Rad's insights into Hebrew Wisdom.

(3) God sees everything
  Prov. 11.21   Be assured, an evil man will not go unpunished /
                but those who are righteous will be delivered.
  Prov. 12.22   Lying lips are an abomination to the LORD /
                but those who act faithfully are his delight.
  Prov. 15.3   The eyes of the LORD are in every place /
                keeping watch on the evil and the good.
  Ton. 839   If you do a wrong deed / you will be struck by
                heaven.

This is one of the main groups in the Bible, but, apart from Tonga 839, there are no African parallels. This is an indication that again we are not dealing with folk wisdom, but with the theological Wisdom of Israel.

(4) The creator of humanity
  Prov. 14.31   He who oppresses a poor man insults his Maker /
                but he who is kind to the needy honours him.
  (also III/6 charity)

---

(41) Plöger, BK, ad.loc., translates: "Beim Menschen (liegen) die Überlegungen des Herzens
    / aber von Jahwe (kommt) die Antwort der Zunge".

Prov. 16.4   The LORD makes everything for its purpose /
            even the wicked for the day of trouble.
(also VII/2 The fate of the wicked)
Prov. 20.12 The hearing ear and the seeing eye /
            the LORD makes them both.
(also VI/5 God's activity)
There are no African parallels. As the few Hebrew examples can easily
be assigned to other topics, I suggest deleting this group.

(5) God's activity in human life

Prov. 12.2   A good man obtains favour from the LORD /
            but a man of evil devices he condemns.
Prov. 14.26 In the fear of the LORD one has strong confidence/
            and his children will have a refuge.
Prov. 15.25 The LORD tears down the house of the proud /
            but he maintains the widow's boundaries.
Mash. p.173 A chance find comes by luck / but that to which one
            is called comes from one's *Mudzimu* (family spirit).
Bag. p.485   The god (*Lubare*) helps you / when you put forth your
            running powers (= self-help).
Hausa 52   The truly contented man comes from Allah.
Ton. 840 ·   Red (or white) garments attract heaven
            (= lightning).
Mal. 1962   The old woman crossing the river:
            it is 'Let God do whatever is good /
            whether I get upset or get across'.

A strong group in Prov. 10–29; in Africa it is not so widespread with the
exception of the Hausa, which may well be due to Islamic influence.

(6) God remains beyond all opposites (Matthew 5.45)

Prov. 22.2   The rich and the poor meet together /
            the LORD is the maker of them all.
(also III/4 poor and rich)
Prov. 29.13 The poor man and the oppressor meet together /
            the LORD gives light to the eyes of both.
(also III/4)
Ton. 885   The ancestor's spirit's plate is one (for all).
Aki. p.219 The enemy of man is not God (= God is just).
Hausa 67   Allah you have no evil /

You make rain fall even on the wizard's garden.

This, too, is probably not an independent group. The African parallels are rather thin on the ground and in the case of the Hausa probably due to Islamic influence.

According to Ruth Finnegan, it is noteworthy that hardly any Bantu proverbs refer to religion, in marked contrast to the West African Hausa and Fulani which belong to Islam. "This may perhaps be connected with the significance of the ancestor cult in many Bantu societies, so that the equivalent of this sort of allusions is made in terms of human experience and activity without reference to a transcendent god or specialist religious activity."[42]

VII The Righteous and the Wicked

(1) Contrast of the mode of existence of the righteous and the wicked
   In Prov. this is a large group with two dozen occurrences:
   Prov. 10.20   The tongue of the righteous is choice silver /
                 the mind of the wicked is of little worth.
   Prov. 11.11   By the blessing of the upright a city is exalted/
                 but it is overthrown by the mouth of the wicked.
   Prov. 12.5   The thoughts of the righteous are just /
                 the counsels of the wicked are treacherous.
   Mal. 102   The righteous are like the long stone of sacrifice /
                 wherever it is placed, all are good.
   Lov. p.286   The well-doer does well unto the well-doer /
                 it is only his despoiler that the despoiler
                 despoils.

(2) Contrast of the fate of the righteous and the wicked
   This again is a large group with three dozen occurrences, concentrated mainly in Prov. 10-14:
   Prov. 10.3   The LORD does not let the righteous go hungry /
                 but he thwarts the craving of the wicked.
   Prov. 11.5   The righteousness of the blameless keeps his way

(42) Finnegan, *Oral Literature*, p.404.

straight /
but the wicked falls by his own wickedness.

Prov. 14.32   The wicked is overthrown through his evil-doing /
but the righteous finds refuge through his integrity.[43]

Mal. 1717   Evil doers: if they are not withered by the day /
they are rotted by the night.

Ton. 782   The good man dies in the bush / the evil one dies
at home.

Section VII is one of the most important in Prov. 10-29. Africa by contrast provides only a few accidental finds. Only two out of 2000 Malagassy proverbs deal with this subject, but in fact they do not contain contrasts. The Tonga proverb is the only one among 1000, and the Lovedu example is really more concerned with the act-consequence relationship.

We may therefore safely conclude that section VII is without parallel in Africa. This control test confirms that the contrast between the mode of existence as well as the fate of the righteous and the wicked is not a concern of folk wisdom, but rather has to be attributed to the theological Wisdom of Israel.

To summarize: The proverbs of Israel and Africa show widespread agreement in sections I-V. In both cases we are dealing with folk proverbs. This means in Claus Westermann's words that "the direct derivation of Israel's Wisdom from the high cultures which surround her becomes questionable. We should rather have to assume that the basic stock of Israelite proverbs goes back to a very distant past ..., the pre- and early history of the tribes."[44]

The absence of sections VI and VII ('God and Man' and 'The Righteous and the Wicked') among the African proverbs shows clearly that Israel under the influence of the YHWH faith has produced a theological reflection of Wisdom which is without parallel among 'primitive' peoples.

(43) Cf. Plöger, BK, ad.loc.
(44) Westermann, "Weisheit im Sprichwort", *Forschung am Alten Testament II*, p.156.

4

Rich and Poor

Peter Doll in his book, *Menschenschöpfung und Weltschöpfung in der alttestamentlichen Weisheit*,[1] investigates the *creation of man* and that *of the world* in Hebrew Wisdom. With regard to the former he comes to the conclusion that the creation of man functions as part of social criticism. There is therefore a close relationship between the sayings concerning the creation of man and those concerning rich and poor. Both are, according to Doll, used by wise and experienced elders in order to defuse conflict and to minimalize social tension.[2]

Following H.W. Wolff, *Amos' geistige Heimat*,[3] Doll attributes these social tensions to the time of the early monarchy and, like Wolff, he regards the Hebrew Wisdom tradition as the root from which criticism of this social situation sprang, both in the Book of Amos and in Prov. 10-29.

With regard to these sayings, Doll[4] sticks his neck out by trying to date them approximately in the middle or late period of the monarchy:

Prov.14.31   He who oppresses a poor man insults his Maker /but he who is kind to the needy honours him, and

Prov.22.2   The rich and the poor meet together /the LORD is the maker of them all.

In my opinion Doll is right in claiming that these proverbs were *used* during the monarchy as part of social criticism, but he is quite wrong when dating their *origin* to the period in question.

By comparing the sayings concerning rich and poor in Prov. 10-29 to those of Africa, it should become obvious that both go back to tribal societies. This implies that Doll's socially responsible elders have to be placed

(1) Stuttgart 1985,
(2) Doll, *Menschenschöpfung*, p.29,
(3) WMANT 18, Neukirchen-Vluyn 1964,
(4) ibid,

in the period of the Judges. Already then, as in the tribal societies of Africa, there was a marked difference between poor and rich. But while tribal societies have a tendency to redress this imbalance, the early capitalism of the Israelite and Judaean monarchy increased class divisions more and more.

The African material I have selected for comparison comes from three large collections (more than 1000 proverbs), those of the Malagasy in Madagascar,[5] the Tonga[6] and the Kundu of Cameroon,[7] and from several smaller ones of the Fante,[8] Bantu,[9] Bavenda,[10] Kafir (2x),[11] Mashona,[12] Chagga,[13] Baganda,[14] Akikuyu,[15] Masai (2x),[16] Nandi,[17] Ewe,[18] and Hausa.[19] The difference between Africa and the Old Testament which immediately springs to mind is the fact that more than a third of the biblical proverbs contrast rich and poor, while only one sixth of the African ones do the same:

Wealth OR Poverty separately:
Old Testament: 38   Africa: 146
Contrast of Rich / Poor:
Old Testament: 21   Africa: 24

(5) J.A. Houlder, *OHABOLANA or Malagasy Proverbs I & II*, Antananarivo 1915/16; French translations by H. Noyer (= Mal.). The explanations of the original collectors and editors appear in brackets (=...).

(6) H.P. Junod and A.A. Jaques, *The Wisdom of the Tonga-Shangaan People*, Cleveland/ Transvaal 1936 (= Ton.).

(7) J. Ittmann, *Sprichwörter der Kundu (Kamerun)*, Berlin 1971 (= Kundu). According to Ittmann, "proverb in Lokundu means *bokana*, a noun which is derived from a verb *kana* 'to be or to become similar'. From this designation it is apparent that proverbs serve for the Mokundu as parables, and this also explains their frequent use in daily life" (p.3).

(8) J.B. Christensen, "The Role of Proverbs in Fante Culture", in E.P. Skinner (ed.), *Peoples and Cultures of Africa*, New York 1973, pp. 509ff (= Fante).

(9) H.P. Junod, *Bantu Heritage*, Johannesburg 1938, pp.46ff (= Bantu),

(10) H.A. Stayt, *The Bavenda*, London 1931, pp.360-61 (= Bav.),

(11) G. McCall, *Kaffir Folk-lore*, 1892 (= Kaf.) and Dudley Kidd, *The Essential Kafir*, London 1904 (= Kaf.2).

(12) C. Bullock, *The Mashona. The Indigenous Natives of S.Rhodesia*, Cape Town and Johannesburg 1927 (= Mash.),

(13) C. Dundas, *Kilimanjaro and its People*, London 1924, pp.341ff (= Chag.),

(14) John Roscoe, *The Baganda*, London 1911 (= Bag.),

(15) C. Cagnolo, *The Akikuyu. The Customs, Traditions and Folklore*, Nyeri/Kenia 1933, pp.214ff (= Aki.),

(16) M. Merker, *Die Masai*, Berlin 1904 (= Mas.) and A.C. Hollis, *The Masai. Their Language and Folklore*, Oxford 1905 (= Masai),

(17) A.C. Hollis, *The Nandi. Their Language and Folklore*, Oxford 1909 = 1969 (= Nandi),

(18) A.B. Ellis, *The EWE-Speaking Peoples*, London 1890 (= Ewe),

(19) R.S. Rattray, *Hausa Folk-lore II*, Oxford 1913, pp.254ff (= Hausa).

This is due to the fact that the Hebrew *parallelismus membrorum* facilitates such a contrast by use of the antithetic parallelism.

Both in the Bible and in Africa wealth is seen as something ambiguous. On the one hand it is a gift of blessing; it is achieved by hard work; it protects in danger, and it leads to honour in society, if the rich man gives liberally. But it can also become a source of danger. The rich man can overreach himself; his wealth can evaporate; false friends can eat it up, and the rich man can become the target of envy and hatred. Good health, a good name, and virtue are to be preferred.

Let us first of all look at the positive aspects of

I)   Wealth.

a)   Blessing and protection for the individual.
   Prov.10.22   The blessing of the LORD makes rich / and he adds no sorrow with it.
   Prov.18.11   A rich man's wealth is his strong city / and like a high wall protecting him.
   Prov.22.4   The reward of humility and the fear of the LORD / is riches and honour and life.
   But in order to have this function of protection and security wealth must not be hastily gotten - and certainly not through greed by dubious means.
   Prov.13.11   Wealth hastily gotten will dwindle / but he who gathers little by little will increase it.
   Prov.28.20   A faithful man will abound with blessings / but he who hastens to be rich will not go unpunished (or better: will not remain guiltless).
   Prov.15.27   He who is greedy for unjust gain makes trouble for his household / but he who hates bribes will live.
   Prov.28.25   A greedy man stirs up strife / but he who trusts in the LORD will be enriched.
   A similarly positive view of wealth is taken by the following African proverbs:
   Ton.28   (= Bantu p.47) A crocodile does not grow thin.(= A rich man can do what he likes).
   Ton.274   A man who has possessions / is not harmed by anything.

Fante p.513   The wealthy man is senior.

Mal.735   Man is the receiver / but riches the giver of blessings.

Mal.759   seems to have the form of a riddle:
Not expected and not looked for / like the honey below
the *vintanina* tree.- Answer = wealth!

Mal.771   It is like having a calf born in the summer / both gladness
and gain.

Bav.36   Rich things seek each other.

The Old Testament warning against hastily gotten wealth is not shared
by the Kundu proverbs of Cameroon:

Kundu 961   Wealth grows overnight.

Kundu 625   Wealth is wealth.(= The achievement of one person is
equal to that of another).

Both biblical and African proverbs seem to be aware of the fact that

b)   wealth is not everything / ambiguous.

Prov.22.1   A good name is to be chosen rather than great riches / and
favour is better than silver or gold.

This is, however, directly contradicted by a Fante proverb with its
matter-of-fact attitude:

Fante p.513   A good name cannot be eaten / it is money that counts.

Almost identical are Prov.10.2 and 11.4:

Prov.10.2   Treasures gained by wickedness do not profit / but
righteousness delivers from death.

Prov.11.4   Riches do not profit in the day of wrath / but righteousness
delivers from death.

Prov.11.28   He who trusts in riches will wither / but the righteous will
flourish like a green leaf.

Kundu 12   Those who follow the rich have enough to eat / but also
enough trouble.

Kundu 1363 Who carries (= is rich) has to bear.

Ton.558   Wealth is bits of roasted meat / the great thing is one's kith
and kin.

Ton.559   Wealth is salt / it just seasons / the important thing is
kindness.

Aki. p.214   Virtue is better than wealth.

Ewe 27   Riches buy slaves / but not life.

Kundu 963 Health in old age is better than wealth.

The rich also have

c)   many friends,

who eat up one's fortune and tend to disappear afterwards.

Próv.19.4   Wealth brings many new friends / but a poor man is deserted by his friend.

Prov.14.20   The poor is disliked even by his neighbour / but the rich has many friends.

Bag. p.486   You have many friends / as long as you are prosperous. Aki. p.224 Many friends empty the pocket. Hausa 18 They pat the cow / before they begin to milk her. Kundu 1195 An elephant has many pieces of meat. (= The rich man's wealth can be tapped).

Common to the Bible and Africa is also the praise of

d) the liberal giver,

although there are warnings that his wealth is not unlimited.

Prov.11.25   A liberal man will be enriched / and one who waters himself will be watered.

Nandi 48   Even if the elephant (= rich man) is big / it does not bear two calves. (= There is a limit to everybody's generosity). Mal.626 It will do no good to have wealth that you will not use (to hoard it only). Ton.26 (= Bantu p.47) Do not beat the crocodile with sand! (= Do not give wealth to those who have it) - a case of coals to Newcastle.

Both the Hebrew and African sages voice a warning that

e) wealth does not protect nor last for ever.

Prov.21.6   The getting of treasure by a lying tongue / is a fleeting vapour and a snare of death.

Prov.27.23+24 Know well the condition of your flocks /and give attention to your herds /for riches do not last for ever /and does a crown endure to all generations?

Bag. p.491   They break unbaked pots. (= Rich wastrels). (ibid) He who cuts the plantain fibre. (= When a wealthy person dies his dependants are scattered). Very similar are the two following Malagasy proverbs:

Mal.737   Money is like a stranger: /it comes today and goes tomorrow. Mal.738 Money does not lie in the road like water: /it comes today, but goes tomorrow.

Mal.740   Wealth is like the hair in the nose: /if much is pulled out / it is painful /if little /it is painful. Mal.756 Salt dropped into the water /it won't return again.-A riddle with the answer = wealth.

Mal.788 Don't keep treasure in a basket with holes. Mal.1930 Don't be as a young man fond of play /life may be long /but a superabundance of wealth won't last. Ton.277 The wealth of the wicked will be scattered by the wind like chaff. Ton.618 To eat one's fill brings ill-luck and famine.(= Power and riches bring poverty after them). Kaf.(2) p.297 Hunger is hidden under sacks of corn.(= Said to people who are vain about their wealth). Bag. p.491 Risk is never absent from those who seek wealth.

There is a group of sayings in Africa concerned with

f) envy and hatred

which the rich man and his wealth arouse. In the Bible such sayings are rare. An exception is perhaps

Prov.28.25 A greedy man stirs up strife /but he who trusts in the LORD will be enriched.

Mal.1430 A tall tree is hated by the wind /and a rich person is hated by other men. Kaf.(2) p.297 The miser is a thief. Aki. p.215 He who has had his fill /becomes thoughtless. Aki. p.216 He who has had his fill /cannot understand what he is told (i.e. the troubles of others). Aki. p.223 The sated person calls the other greedy. Mas. p.220 Few people are good / when we want something (from them). Chag.15 Your wealth is your destruction.(= Riches create envy; if you have little to covet you have few enemies).

A further African group of proverbs deals with the idea that what is needed for acquiring wealth is

g) hard effort.

The Bible makes the same point with its humorous sayings concerning the sluggard (Prov.22.13; also 10.26; 15.19; 20.4 et al.). In two Malagasy proverbs the message is put over both straight and metaphorically:

Mal.658 Continue long enough /and you will grow rich. Mal.659 Long feet will find food.

A third and fourth one use a comparison:[20]

Mal.748 Even the locust cannot be captured without an effort / much less riches. Mal.765 Gather riches as you gather cow-dung (for fuel): /whether little or much /put it all in the basket.

(20) C. Westermann, *The Parables of Jesus in the Light of the Old Testament*, Edinburgh 1990 (ET of *Vergleiche und Gleichnisse im Alten und Neuen Testament*, Stuttgart 1984).

Hausa 11   It is the rainy season that gives wealth. Kundu 39 You do
not get wealth by coughing. (= Visitors cough before the
door – If you want to gain something, you need to make
an effort beforehand).

Now we need to look at the biblical and African proverbs concerning

II) Poverty.

Both in Africa and in the Bible there seem to be roughly the same number
of proverbs concerning poverty as there are concerning wealth, a fact which
is further supported by group III contrasting rich and poor.

But while the Old Testament's view of poverty is ambiguous – it is
regarded as great hardship, but the poor man, too, is God's creature and he
also has his qualities – in Africa poverty is nearly always considered a great
evil. The biblical appeal to give alms to the needy is also not matched by
African proverbs.

This points to two things: (1) Due to poor living conditions, poverty in
Africa is much greater than it was in Israel during the period of the Judges.
And (2) the concern for the poor in Israel is strongly formed by her faith in
YHWH. While in Africa religion plays no great part in proverbs,[21] the
concern for the poor (stranger, orphan, and widow) was central to Israel's
faith. This could not remain unreflected in her proverbs.

Let us first look at

a) the positive view of poverty

and of the poor. On the basis of the Hebrew doctrine of the creation of
man, rooted in the Individual Lament and functioning as part of social
criticism,[22] it was emphasized that the poor as creatures were considered
equal to the rich. Both had the same maker:

Prov.14.31   He who oppresses a poor man insults his Maker /but he
who is kind to the needy honours him. Prov.17.5 He who
mocks the poor insults his Maker /he who is glad at
calamity will not go unpunished.

Hence the admonition:

Prov.22.22   Do not rob the poor, because he is poor /or crush the
afflicted at the gate (in a court case).

(21) cf. Ruth Finnegan, *Oral Literature in Africa*, Oxford 1970, p.404,
(22) cf. Doll, *Menschenschöpfung*, pp.15-29,

This is indeed the tradition on which Amos bases himself.[23] Cf. also Isa.1.17.

Prov.16.26   A worker's appetite works for him /his mouth urges him on. Prov.19.22 What is desired in a man is loyalty /and a poor man is better than a liar.

There is little in Africa to match these biblical statements about the poor. Perhaps

Mal.1477   Angry about one you love /you go off in a passion /angry about being poor /you work at night. Kundu 731 The poor man's hen breeds even on an evil day. Mal.1458 Poverty is no reproach.- A rather isolated statement.

Some comfort for the poor is, however, provided by the community, especially in Cameroon:

Kundu 456   There is no poverty in a settlement.(= While the individual may be poor, his clan will support him). Kundu 1251 A baby does not get hungry because of poverty.(= If you have somebody who cares for you, you will not be in need). Kundu 1181 "I have nothing" is not ashamed.

But, apart from these few positive Kundu and Malagasy proverbs, dominant in Africa is

b)   the negative view of poverty,

which can also be found in the Old Testament. Poverty can be caused by idleness, the seeking of too much pleasure or the failure to obey instructions. It can also come unawares.

Prov.19.15   Slothfulness casts into a deep sleep /and an idle person will suffer hunger. Prov.20.4 The sluggard does not plough in the autumn /he will seek at harvest and have nothing. Prov.21.17 He who loves pleasure will be a poor man /he who loves wine and oil will not be rich.-A synthetic parallelism.

Prov.23.20+21   Be not among winebibbers /or among gluttonous eaters of meat /for the drunkard and the glutton will come to poverty /and drowsiness will clothe a man with rags. Prov.13.18 Poverty and disgrace come to him who ignores instruction / but he who heeds reproof is honoured. Prov.24.34 Poverty will come upon you like a robber /and want like an armed man.

This negative view of poverty is much more widespread in Africa.

(23) Amos 4.1; 5.7,11,15,24; 8.4; Doll, *Menschenschöpfung*, p.29,

Mal.1448   A poor man living by the side of the market /his wishes are
             many /but his means are scanty.–Similarly Mal.1449 A
             poor man going to market thrusts his fist in his mouth.
             Mal.1454 (When) the poor leave home in the morning /
             people think it is to steal /and when they leave in the
             evening /people think it is to stop (others on the road).
             Mal.1455 A poor person looking at public games /he takes
             home tears. (= Brings home his poverty to him). Mal.1463
             A youth with a torn dress /is one of those who mix with
             others /but he feels ashamed. Mal.1466 He has a body but
             no riches. Mal.1468 He has no basket to put (things) into
             /like a dog. Mal.1478 Punished by a little pride /he is
             injured by poverty. Mal.1480 Dirty dress buying meat /he
             is not known by the people to be in earnest. Mal.1934 The
             poor man with a bald head is not called 'venerable'.
             Ton.155 A dog cannot choose its own place.(= A poor
             man cannot choose his own way). Ton.283 (= Bantu p.49)
             A skeleton has no flesh.(= You will not find meat on a
             skeleton, nor wealth in a poor man).

Two Fante proverbs point out that the poor receive no justice in court:

Fante p.513   A poor man cannot win a court case. (ibid) The poor man's
             plea receives hurried treatment.
Bantu p.48   A dog's sweat remains in its own hair.(= The poor man's
             work does not profit him). Mash. p.174 That which is on
             a poor man /is on a slippery place.(= From him that has not
             ...). Bag. p.491 I had a number of friends /before calamity
             befell me. Aki. p.225 The generosity of the poor disappears
             from his heart.(= A poor man has nothing to give). Nandi
             11 He thought of milk during the hunt.(= is apt to think
             of the days of plenty). Ewe 6 A poor man cannot become
             a priest. Ewe 61 An empty hand does not go to market.
             Hausa 31 The boy wants to marry /but at their (his) house
             there is no more.(= He has no money). Hausa 119 A poor
             man has no friends. Kundu 24 A poor man is not greeted
             like a sick man.(= The poor and the sick both need help;
             but the one is avoided while the other is visited): Kundu
             323 A poor man's house is reluctantly entered in. Kundu
             891 A poor man does not know shame. Kundu 1233 An
             orphan does not put a large rod into running streams.(= A

poor man cannot stand up to respected people). Mal.777
It is more easy to scatter than to collect. Mal.778 Got
wrongly and spent foolishly. Mal.783 When there is no
more money /there is no more finery. Mal.997 Poverty
won't allow him to lift up his head /and dignity won't allow
him to bow it down.

Three Malagasy proverbs point out that litigation can lead to poverty,
even if you win your court case:

Mal.1083   Love law and lose money. Mal.1084 Let it be talk /for if it
is going to be law /the property is wasted. Mal.1085 A long
suit / and poor recompense.

Mal.1460   It is distress that clothes a man with rags. Mal.1461 Having
little money and eat bad food.Ton.256 (= Bantu p.48)
Authority (wealth) is never plentiful /but poverty is.(=
Even though a chief is rich, he is not satisfied with his riches,
while the poor man knows poverty and must be content
with it). Ton.279 (= Bantu p.49) Poverty is bewitchment.[24]
(= A really poor man has no means of leading a tolerable
life. He is like a bewitched person). Ton.290 The stick
which is far away /does not kill a snake.(= Riches far away
do not help you when you are in trouble). Kundu 319
Poverty and audacity: / a single person. Kundu 753
Poverty does not befall stones.- Only people! Kundu 898
One season does not end poverty.(= To achieve something
you have to try more than once). Kundu 96 Even the
owners have nothing left.

c)   Alms and charity

Sayings concerning alms and charity are rare in Africa. When they occur
in the Old Testament, the motivation for alms giving is either purely
utilitarian or strongly religious. Both occur side by side, and it is not possible
to say that one is older than the other. The concern for one's poor brother
is characteristic of tribal societies, but also one of the basic elements of Israel's
faith in YHWH.

Prov.28.27   He who gives to the poor will not want /but he who hides
his eyes will get many a curse. Prov.19.17 He who is kind
to the poor lends to the LORD /and he will repay him for
his deed. Prov.14.21 He who despises his neighbour is a

(24) cf. also Sir Edward Evans-Pritchard, *Witchcraft, Oracles, and Magic among the Azande*,
Oxford 1976,

sinner /but happy is he who is kind to the poor. Prov.21.13
He who closes his ear to the cry of the poor /will himself
cry out and not be heard. Prov.22.9 He who has a bountiful
eye will be blessed /for he shares his bread with the poor.
Prov.29.7 A righteous man knows the rights of the poor /
a wicked man does not understand such knowledge.-A late
and general saying reflecting probably the second temple
community. Mal.774 Spilt grains of rice are the friends of
the fowls.

But there is also a warning against charity:

Mal.949   Don't depend on a brother's wealth.

III) Contrast between Rich and Poor

These sayings contrast the lives of the rich and the poor, how the one is
affected by his wealth and the other by his poverty. The *tov ... min* (better
... than) sayings and many other proverbs place the virtuous poor above the
corrupt rich. And the sayings based on the creation of man emphasize the
equality of both as creatures before their Maker.[25]

a) The positive view of poverty

Prov.28.6   Better is a poor man who walks in his integrity/than a rich
              man who is perverse in his ways.-
              This *tov ... min* saying is identical with Prov.19.1, if we are
              allowed to read as the last word '*ashir* (rich) for *kesil* (fool).
              But Plöger rejects this emendation.[26]

Prov.15.16   Better a little with the fear of the LORD /than great
              treasure and trouble with it. Prov.16.8 Better is a little with
              righteousness /than great revenues with injustice.

Similar to Prov.15.16;16.8 is

Masai 70   Better is to be poor and live long /than rich and die young.

Prov.22.2   The rich and the poor meet together /the LORD is the
              maker of them all. Prov.29.13 The poor man and the
              oppressor meet together /the LORD gives light to the eyes
              of both. Prov.28.11 A rich man is wise in his own eyes /

---

(25) Doll, *Menschenschöpfung*, pp.15-29,

(26) O.Plöger, *Sprüche Salomos (Proverbia)*, Biblischer Kommentar XVII, Neukirchen-Vluyn
     1984, ad loc.

but a poor man who has understanding will find him out.
Wealth and poverty can be deceptive:

Prov.13.7   One man pretends to be rich, yet has nothing /another
pretends to be poor, yet has great wealth. Prov.28.22 A
miserly man hastens after wealth /and does not know that
want will come upon him.

But the rich can also be dependent on the poor:

Kundu 821   The dwarf antelope (who lives close by the water) has
begged water from the monkey (who lives on trees).(=
Sometimes even a rich man needs the help of a poor one).
Cf. also Kundu 1113 The fish came to the bird in order to
beg. Kundu 830 It is not good, if a village is full of rich
people.(= Said to comfort the poor).

b)   The neutral view of wealth and poverty

While the above proverbs tried to show the positive aspects of poverty,
the following three observe the status quo from a neutral perspective:

Prov.10.15   The rich man's wealth is his strong city /the poverty of the
poor is their ruin. Prov.13.8 The ransom of a man's life is
his wealth /but a poor man 'remains deaf to threats' – as he
cannot pay anyway.[27] Prov.11.24 One man gives freely,
yet grows all the richer /another withholds what he should
give, and only suffers want.

c)   The negative view of poverty

The following proverbs attribute poverty to sloth and idleness. The poor
man has brought his misery upon himself. This negative view of poverty is
also typical of Africa.

Prov.10.4   A slack hand causes poverty /but the hand of the diligent
makes rich. Prov.28.19 He who tills his land will have
plenty of bread/but he who follows worthless pursuits will
have plenty of poverty. Prov.12.27 A slothful man will not
catch his prey /but the diligent man will get precious
wealth. Prov.21.5 The plans of the diligent lead surely to
abundance /but everyone who is hasty comes only to want.
Prov.22.7 The rich rules over the poor /and the borrower
is slave to the lender. Prov.18.23 The poor use entreaties
/but the rich answer roughly.

The following is hardly a folk proverb, but the result of theological
reflection:

(27) after Plöger, BK, ad loc.

Prov.13.21   Misfortune pursues sinners /but prosperity rewards the righteous.

Mal.776   If you are clever, go gather money /but if you are not clever, you gather fuel. Mal.1426 He who has riches is a prince /but he who has not is a robber. Mal.1450 A poor man talking to a rich man /when he gets home he burns the house fastening (= piece of wood that fastens the door).Mal.1452 The poor are not companions for the rich. Mal.1622 The poor are fools /but the rich seem wise. Ton.817 To give is to save /to be mean is to throw away.(= If you give liberally, you will also be given when in need). cf. Prov.19.17. Mas. p.220 A rich man has many friends / a poor man has nothing.Masai 33 A man does not know / when he is well off /it is only when he is poor /that he remembers the days of plenty. Hausa 29 (If you have) a big log /you have a fire beside you all night /if a stick /then ashes only. Hausa 117 Things (wealth) is the man /if you have nothing, no one loves you. Kundu 1395 Idleness and poverty /industry and wealth.

This negative view of poverty is dominant in Africa.

IV) Inheritance

A small group of sayings deals with inherited wealth:

Prov.13.22   A good man leaves an inheritance to his children's children /but the sinner's wealth is laid up for the righteous. Prov.20.21 An inheritance gotten hastily in the beginning /will in the end not be blessed. Prov.28.8 He who augments his wealth by interest and increase /gathers it for him who is kind to the poor.–Applying perhaps to a father and his son.[28] Prov.19.14 House and wealth are inherited from the fathers/but a prudent wife is from the LORD. Mal.1432 A rich miser hoards up for those who bury him. Ton.463 Eat the mealies of the dead /but go on ploughing.(= Do not put your trust in an inheritance, if you do not work. It will soon vanish). Fante p.515 It does not take long for

(28) cf. Ezek.18.5-9,10-13

a tree to grow /then it sprang from a tree stump. (= wealth inherited). (ibid) All mushrooms grow in the same place / but some are eaten /and others are not. (= debts inherited). (ibid) If you depend on someone else for breakfast /go without food.(= Do not depend on an inheritance). Kaf. p.190 You drink out of an old cup. (= wealth inherited).Ewe 31 A poor man's son does not brag. Kundu 44 One does not leave debts for the funeral dance. Kundu 1065 The rich man does not use up his wealth (but passes it on as an inheritance). Kundu 1257 The child of a free man spends the fortune of his father.(= Children of well-to-do fathers are not used to work).

These sayings are ambiguous in so far as they praise those who make provision for future generations, but also warn against too much reliance on an inheritance.

V) Loans, debts and surety

While the biblical proverbs warn against the giving of surety in particular for strangers, the African ones are mainly concerned with debts and their consequences.

Prov.11.15   He who gives surety for a stranger will smart for it / but he who hates surety is secure. Prov.17.18 A man without sense gives a pledge /and becomes surety in the presence of his neighbour. Prov.20.16 (= 27.13) Take a man's garment when he has given surety for a stranger /and hold him in pledge when he gives surety for foreigners. Prov.22.7b The borrower is the slave of the lender. Prov.22.26 Be not one of those who give pledges /and become surety for debts.

Mal.793   Don't waste rice /for it is difficult to borrow any in planting-time.Mal.966 If you could not borrow any rice once /don't bury the rice-basket. Mal.1309 A rag lent in place of something else: /the one who owns the worthless thing says much about taking care of it. Mal.1310 Don't borrow a garment as a thief does. Mal.1311 To wear loosely a borrowed garment /and, on arriving, get it stripped off by the owner. Ton.622 The wise man has only one helping /the fool many.(= When a person borrows something and does not return it, nobody will ever lend him anything again).Ton.728 The borrower of a little cloth wears it with care. Bag. p.485 A borrower only seeks you in order that he may borrow / and not repay you. Hausa 116 To borrow is sweet (easy) /the day of payment is hard. Ton.419 Debt is (like) a blanket.(= Nobody can live without debts. They are like the blanket of a traveller). Ton.420 Debt is dirt.(= Debt comes back like dirt). Kundu 962 Someone who is really rich has no debts. Kundu 99 If a debt of five shillings is demanded of you /and you have five shillings at home /they are not yours. Kundu 223 When you have paid your debts /you can safely walk the main street. Kundu 311 Debts grow old /but they do not pass away! (Cameroon law). Kundu 312 Even if debts exist ever so long /on the day they are to be paid /they are as good as new. Kundu 611 Cast off the dust and cross (the river) on the trunk of a tree.(= Pay your debts, and you have piece and quiet). Kundu 746 The blood revenge which leaves one person alive is not yet over.(= As long as the creditor is alive, the debt has to be paid). Kundu 796 Debts which have grown never end. Kundu 797 To be in debt to a woman /is not good for a man. Kundu 971 He who gives pledges /has sold his mother.(= The multitude of debts gets him into deeper and deeper trouble).

Looking through all groups of proverbs concerning rich and poor again, the many common features make it safe for us to say that both the African and the biblical material originated in a tribal society, i.e. in Israel during the period of the Judges.

There are, however, different features which suggest to me that the biblical proverbs have been worked over under the influence of the YHWH faith, what Doll calls *Aktualisierung und Neuinterpretation* during the social crisis at the time of the prophet Amos.[29] The concern of Israel's faith for the poor, the orphan and the widow could not be ignored by her proverbial wisdom.

Compared to Africa, the Hebrew proverbs place greater emphasis on alms giving. They also take a more positive view of poverty by placing virtue

(29) Doll, *Menschenschöpfung*, p.29,

above wealth. By appealing to the creation of each individual human being by YHWH, the poor were able to hold their ground in relation to their rich exploiters. This reflects the ethos of an egalitarian tribal society,[30] but could easily be re-applied to the struggles during the 8th century B.C. in Israel and Judah.

Our results are therefore in agreement with Norman Whybray's study: "Such evidence as is to be found here suggests that their settings are predominantly those of the life of the small farmers farming their own land (and perhaps, to some extent, of an urban proletariat). It is strongly implied that only constant hard work allied with common sense and a resistance to temptation to fritter away one's substance on inessentials and self-indulgence can stave off the threat of poverty. While some of the warnings would no doubt constitute sound advice if offered to members of any social class, they would undoubtedly be far more relevant to the circumstances of the manual worker than of the relatively secure upper class."[31]

(30) N.K. Gottwald, *The Tribes of Yahweh. A Sociology of the Religion of Liberated Israel 1250-1050 B.C.E.*, London 1980,

(31) R.N. Whybray, *Wealth and Poverty in the Book of Proverbs*, JSOT Suppl 99, Sheffield 1990, p.31.

5

Law, Crime and Justice

The reason for the fact that the Old Testament has so few proverbs referring to the above topics is obviously the existence of the many legal corpora of the Pentateuch. But still, some proverbs can be found.

We have already treated among the Royal and Court sayings those proverbs which make the point that the king's throne has to be based on justice and equal treatment of all his subjects (Prov.16.10; 20.8; 29.4,14).

Among the remainder those proverbs extolling honest evidence and warning against the false witness are particularly noticeable:

Prov.12.17   He who speaks the truth gives honest evidence /but a false witness utters deceit. Prov.19.5 (19.9) A false witness will not go unpunished /and he who utters lies will not escape (will perish). Prov.21.28 A false witness will perish /but the word of a man who hears will endure. Prov.24.28+29 Be not a witness against your neighbour without cause /and do not deceive with your lips /Do not say, "I will do to him as he has done to me /I will pay the man back for what he has done." Prov.25.18 A man who bears false witness against his neighbour /is like a club, or a sword, or a sharp arrow.

Prov.28.24   He who robs his father or his mother /and says, "That is no transgression" /is a companion of a man who destroys. Prov.29.24 The partner of a thief hates his own life /he hears the curse, but discloses nothing.

The two following sayings contain ancient prohibitions, but their second verse is a later theological expansion (for ...):

Prov.23.10+11   Do not remove an ancient landmark /or enter the field of the fatherless /(for their redeemer is strong /he will plead their cause against you). Prov.24.15+16 Lie not in wait as a wicked man against the dwelling of the righteous /do not violence to his home /(for the righteous man falls seven times, and rises again /but the wicked are overthrown by calamity).

Prov.24 + 25   contain two large admonitions. In both cases we have left the realm of the folk proverb.

Prov.24.23b-26

23b: Partiality in judging is not good. 24: He who says to the wicked, "You are innocent" /will be cursed by the people, abhorred by the nations / 25: but those who rebuke the wicked will have delight /and a good blessing will be upon them. 26: He who gives a right answer /kisses the lips.

Prov.25.8-10

8: Do not go hastily to court /for what will you do in the end /when your neighbour puts you to shame? 9: Argue your case with your neighbour himself /and do not disclose another's secret / 10: lest he who hears you bring shame upon you /and your ill repute have no end.

Erhard Gerstenberger in his book, *Wesen und Herkunft des "apodiktischen Rechts"*,[1] argued for a clan wisdom background for Israel's apodictic law. H.-J. Hermisson[2] was able to demonstrate that such clan wisdom was not that of nomads, but that of sedentary farmers. But as the Old Testament provides so little evidence for the origin of legal standards in the clan wisdom of sedentary farmers, let us turn to African tribal societies to see whether in their case the wisdom background for legal standards and maxims can be established.

Ruth Finnegan[3] points out the frequent use of proverbs in oratory. This makes them particularly suitable for law cases or disputes. They are often introduced at the crucial moment of an argument and thereby influence the actual court decisions. "Counsellors and judges also use proverbs to comment obliquely on the conduct of those involved, often with implied advice or rebuke. ... People are rebuked for their wrong behaviour in court and reminded allusively that what they are doing falls into some general category they too disapprove of. Telling lies, for instance, only makes matters worse."[4]

(1)   WMANT 20, Neukirchen-Vluyn 1965,
(2)   *Studien zur israelitischen Spruchweisheit*, WMANT 28, Neukirchen-Vluyn 1968, pp.81-92,
(3)   *Oral Literature in Africa*, Oxford 1970, pp.408f,
(4)   Finnegan, *Oral Literature*, p.408,

According to Ruth Finnegan, proverbs are frequently used "to smooth over a disagreement or bring a dispute to a close....a difficult law case is often ended by the public citation of an apt proverb which performs much the same generalizing function as citing legal precedents in other societies. Some of these might be classed as juridical axioms and maxims, but many in fact succeed just because the attempt at reconciliation is oblique and through an analogy rather than a straightforward injunction. The contenders are not only brought to view the dispute in a wider perspective (and thus be more ready to come to terms), but this is conveyed in a tactful and allusive way."[5] Court cases, therefore, provide many opportunities for the use of proverbs.

Following the lead of Carole R. Fontaine,[6] we might first of all look at cases of proverb performance. The best anthropological study in this respect known to me is, "The Role of Proverbs in a Nigerian Judicial System", by John C. Messenger jr.[7]

Messenger's study is devoted to the Anang, the second largest of six Ibibio-speaking tribes of southeastern Nigeria. He investigates the use of proverbs in court, and in particular how this rhetorical device is affecting the course of Anang justice. The Anang are not unlike Israel during the period of the Judges in so far that they possess no centralized political organization. The important social grouping is not so much the sub-tribe or the clan, but the patrilineage, called *ekpuk*, which corresponds to the Hebrew *beth abh*. Messenger comments: "The largest social grouping is the patrilineage, known as *ekpuk*, composed of both nuclear and extended families inhabiting a continuous tract of territory in the village. Each family lives in a compound surrounded by forest, bush, and land belonging to the head and farmed by his wives and children."[8]

As a result of British colonial administration traditional courts have disappeared at tribal level, but they still function in the village, the patrilineage, and the family. "The head of the family and, if they reside in the compound, his adult brothers and sons form the family court, which convenes in the house of the compound leader at sunset on the day an offense is committed. The crimes most commonly tried are quarreling among wives" - cf. Sarah/Hagar, Leah/Rachel, and Hannah/Peninnah in the Old Testament - "cruelty toward wives, disobedience of children, and petty stealing within the family group. The patrilineage *esop*" (= court)

(5) Finnegan, *Oral Literature*, p.409,

(6) *Traditional Sayings in the Old Testament*, Sheffield 1982,

(7) *Southwestern Journal of Anthropology* (= *SWJA*) 15, 1959, pp.64-73.

(8) Messenger, *SWJA* 15, p.64,

"meets weekly in a court building located in a small square central to the area inhabited by the kin-group. Presided over by the *ekpuk* head, this body consists of family leaders and sometimes of old men who do not hold this position but who have high prestige. Most of the cases brought before the tribunal can be tried either here or in the village court, depending on whether the principals are from the same or from different patrilineages. Chief among the offenses in this category are theft, assault with a deadly weapon, adultery, and causing an unmarried girl to become pregnant."[9]

Messenger outlines court procedure, using the village court as an example. This court consists of the older men of the village and a smaller number of older women. Once the presiding member has introduced the case under consideration, the plaintiff stands up before the justices, called *ekpe ikpe*, and presents his grievance. He does this without assistance of a lawyer and sometimes speaks for a whole hour, before he gives way to the defendant who adopts the same procedure. When the court itself initiates a case, the chief justice speaks as the plaintiff – a procedure familiar from Deutero-Isaiah (Isa.41.1-5; 43.8-13; 44.6-8 et al.). "The *ekpe ikpe* and those in the audience pay rapt attention to the litigants as they deliver their talks, and outbursts of applause mark the course of a well-presented accusation or defense. Listeners are especially appreciative of an original or little known proverb that captures their imagination and is cleverly introduced at a crucial moment."[10]

After the speeches by plaintiff and defendant both are questioned, first of all by each other, then by the members of the court. Character witnesses are brought at this stage. If an oath is sworn, the trial must be postponed until the results of the oath can be ascertained. "When the chief justice decides that sufficient evidence has been introduced, he seeks the opinions of important old men as to the innocence or guilt of the defendant and retires with his colleagues to ponder a decision, returning with them to announce the verdict they have agreed upon."[11]

Messenger calls this system democratic. The evidence is examined with great care and the chief justice normally seeks a consensus among the elders and the members of court.

Messenger reports the case of a chronic thief who was accused of robbery. "The plaintiff aroused considerable antagonism toward the defendant early in the trial by employing the following proverb: 'If a dog plucks palm

(9) Messenger, *SWJA* 15, p.65,
(10) Messenger, *SWJA* 15, p.66,
(11) Messenger, ibid.

fruits from a cluster, he does not fear the porcupine.' A cluster from the oil palm tree contains numerous sharp needles that make handling it extremely hazardous, therefore a dog known to pick palm fruits certainly would be unafraid to touch a porcupine. The maxim implies that the accused is the logical suspect since he was a known thief and lived close to the person who was robbed, and many in the audience regarded the trial as a mere formality. His guilt came to appear doubtful, however, in the light of the evidence produced during the proceedings, and just before the *ekpe ikpe* were to retire he presented an adage that was instrumental in gaining his acquittal: 'A single partridge flying through the bush leaves no path.' Partridges usually travel close to the ground in coveys and can be followed by the trail of bent and broken grass they leave behind. In using this proverb the accused likened himself to a single bird, without sympathizers to lend him support, and called upon the tribunal to disregard the sentiments of those in attendance and to overlook his past misdemeanors and judge the case as objectively as possible."[12]

Messenger reports a further case in which four proverbs were used at crucial stages during the proceedings, one each by the plaintiff and the defendant and two by the chief judge. A person was accused of assaulting a former friend with a machete during a heated argument. The plaintiff used the proverb 'Something happened to the smoke which caused it to enter the bush and become mist'. By using this proverb, "the plaintiff wanted the court to know that he disliked bringing charges against the defendant in the light of their former close association, but was compelled to do so because of the severity of the attack."[13]

The accused countered this by attempting "to show the justices that, although posing as a friend, the plaintiff was in reality a jealous enemy who had chosen this means to discredit him, ending his expose with the adage 'A leopard conceals his spots'. ... Thus the plaintiff was pictured as a dangerous foe hiding his true motives under the guise of friendship."[14]

When the evidence was inconclusive, the presiding judge "appraised the case with the proverb 'If an animal resembles a palm fruit cluster, how can it be butchered?' By this he meant that at this point in the hearing the evidence was so inconclusive that the *ekpe ikpe* would be unable to reach a verdict, just as an animal possessing the needles of a cluster would be difficult to handle."[15]

(12) Messenger, *SWJA* 15, pp.68f,
(13) Messenger, *SWJA* 15, p.69,
(14) Messenger, ibid.
(15) Messenger, *SWJA* 15, pp.69f,

In order to come to a conclusion the court was forced to put the plaintiff under oath. "The chief justice admonished the plaintiff and his supporters with the maxim 'If you visit the home of the toads, stoop' when they expressed their unwillingness to take oaths, thereby forfeiting the case."[16]

In an other case reported by Messenger a boy was accused of impregnating an unmarried girl. His father was called as a character witness, but seemed reluctant to support his son. He had in fact previously punished the boy for sexual practices and the telling of lies. "He told the court, he considered his son capable of having committed the act for which he was accused and ended his testimony by using the precept 'The *nsosok*" (= smallest bird in the region) "said she was ashamed of the small size of her offspring'.... In employing this maxim, the father revealed his lack of faith in his son's claims and the great shame he felt at making this admission publicly."[17]

The boy was finally convicted on the strength of a proverb used by the girl's father when the latter gave evidence: 'The *ekenuk* (= small rat) tried to eat as much as the *okono* (= large rat) and his stomach burst'. "The girl's parents likened the boy to the small variety and a married man to the large one; the youth is about to suffer for an act that only a married man is eligible to perform with his spouse."[18]

These examples given show cases of proverb performance in indigenous Anang courts. Messenger's field work demonstrates clearly the impact of proverb usage on the decisions of these courts. The following list gives those Anang proverbs the usage of which was observed by Messenger[19] during trials:

Anang 1   If a dog plucks palm fruits from a cluster /he does not fear a porcupine.

Anang 2   A single partridge flying through the bush leaves no path.

Anang 3   Something happened to the smoke /which caused it to enter the bush and become mist.

Anang 4   A leopard conceals his spots.

Anang 5   If an animal resembles a palm fruit cluster /how can it be butchered?

Anang 6   If you visit the home of the toads / stoop.

Anang 7   The *nsosok* said she was ashamed of the small size of her offspring.

(16) Messenger, *SWJA* 15, p.70,
(17) Messenger, ibid.
(18) Messenger, ibid.
(19) Messenger, *SWJA* 15, pp.72f,

Anang 8   The *ekenuk* tried to eat as much as the *okono* /and his
            stomach burst.
Anang 9   When the fire burned the dog /it also burned the hunter
            holding the rope attached to the neck of the dog.
Anang 10   Overeating destroys the soul.
Anang 11   The crayfish is bent /because it is sick.

One glance at the above collection shows surprisingly, but clearly, that
none of these proverbs have any legal content. Most of them could be
classified under the heading 'human nature'. In this case it would appear that
the Anang proverbs are not used to quote judicial precedent, but rather that
they have the function of supporting one's own case and of undermining
that of one's opponent. They are also used in support of procedural
decisions by the chief justice and in order to achieve a consensus among the
members of the court.

But there are other African proverbs which address themselves directly
to the topics 'law, crime, justice', e.g. the legal maxims of the Tswana of
Bechuanaland.[20]

A group of 30 proverbs collected by Schapera deals with basic principles
of Tswana law:

Tswana 1   The chief's word is law.
Tswana 3   Manhood is one thing /chieftainship another.(= people
            must respect their elders, but rank takes precedence over
            age, and even old men must respect those of higher birth).
Tswana 4   The chief is a little god /no evil must be spoken of him.
Tswana 5   The head is the chief's.(= he alone is entitled to impose
            capital punishment).
Tswana 7   Cattle belong to the chief /and so do people.(= he controls
            not only his subjects but also their wealth).
Tswana 10   One's parent is one's god.
Tswana 11   The child who does not heed his father's law /will feel that
            of the vultures.
Tswana 12   The first wife's children are the seniors (= they take
            precedence over the children of other wives).
Tswana 13   It is the custom for children to be shared.(= In the case of
            divorce young children accompany their mother, but they
            remain under their father's control and return to him when
            old enough).
Tswana 14   An illegitimate child belongs to its mother's home.(= its

(20) I. Schapera, "Tswana legal Maxims", *Africa* 36, 1966, pp.121-134 = Tswana.

genitor has no rights over it unless he afterwards marries the woman).

Tswana 16   Bridewealth has no price.(= Its amount is not a matter for discussion, the boy's people giving as much as they wish and can afford).-Just the opposite would be true among the Nuer.[21]

Tswana 17   One's cross-cousin is one's spouse.

Tswana 20   Relationship by marriage does not decay.(= A man once married into a family is always regarded as its 'son-in-law', even in case of divorce, so long as he has not taken back his *bogadi* = bridewealth).

Tswana 21   A kinsman begets (or bears) for a barren person.(= A younger sister becomes the 'womb' of a barren elder sister; an impotent husband, similarly, asks a younger brother or brother's son to beget children for him by his wife).

Tswana 24   A field is a woman's concern /a man's is the cattle-kraal.(= a family's cattle are controlled by the husband, its crops by the wife).

Tswana 26   Inheritance goes in order (of seniority).(= to the sons of a second wife if there are none by the first, and to a man's next younger brother if he has no sons at all).

Tswana 28   A dead man's word is not transgressed.(= used especially when an eldest son who has been formally disinherited lays claim to the estate after his father's death).

Tswana 30   A person sucks (or drinks) the milk of the cow he herds.(= A herdsman ... is entitled to the milk of the animals in his care).

Many Tswana proverbs relate to the judicial process itself; "they state, as it were, rules of procedure rather than substance."[22]

Tswana 31   We look not at the person /but at the offence.

Tswana 32   It is not 'Hunger that selects' /it is 'Spears the killers of princes'.(= whereas usually only poor people die of famine, everybody is subject to the penalties of the law).

The chief is not above the law:

Tswana 34   The law is blind /it even eats its owner.

Tswana 35   The law is a lion /it bites the great man too.

(21) Sir Edward Evans-Pritchard, *Kinship and Marriage among the Nuer*, Oxford 1951 = 1990, pp.74ff,

(22) Schapera, *Africa* 36, p.125,

Tswana 37   The gadfly on the back is slapped /that on the belly is fumbled.(= One is lenient with an offending kinsman, but hard on an outsider).

Tswana 38   A *legwane* (= uninitiated youth) is a dog and never sued.(= he is normally dealt with by his own people).

Tswana 40   One doesn't pursue a snake into its hole.(= If you assault someone in his home instead of taking him to court, you are punished more severely than usual, and if you yourself suffer injury there the court will give you no satisfaction).

The following deal with procedure and evidence:

Tswana 43   A wrong does not decay /it is meat that decays.

Tswana 44   Wounds (= assault cases) are prosecuted while they are still fresh.

Tswana 45   A belly is sued for while still a belly.(= if a woman is seduced, action must be taken against her lover while she is still pregnant).

Tswana 46   A fault is reported to its owners.(= to the offender's senior kinsmen).

Tswana 48   When a dog steals /it is given to its owner (to deal with).

Tswana 50   One does not go to the chief for someone else.(= A litigant should appeal in person to the chief against the verdict of a lower court).

Tswana 51   When a child cries for a starling /give it to him.(= If a man clearly in the wrong wants to appeal, people quote this at him, meaning thereby, Go if you insist, though it will be futile).

According to Schapera, the Tswana believe that only the chief can really do them justice:

Tswana 53   The chief is a doctor.(= When we take a case to court, we say we are going to be cured ..., and if the case is settled by the chief himself we are satisfied).

Tswana 54   The owner (is the one who) smites on the forehead.

Tswana 55   The thief is the man carrying the burden.(= the one found in possession of the stolen goods; but there is also the implication that he must be caught with the goods, mere suspicion or hearsay not being enough).

Tswana 56   A man does not skin an ox by himself.(= He usually gets others to help him, so if he is found with much meat, though none of his neighbours had helped him skin and cut up a dead animal of his own, the presumption is that he had stolen and killed the beast).

Tswana 57   The dogs see the pig that is in the rear.(= when a girl becomes pregnant the most recent of her lovers must be held responsible).

Tswana 58   What is seized (or beset) by two dogs /has no strength.=

Tswana 59   Count twice surpasses count once.(= double evidence condemns).

The following proverbs deal with compensation for injuries and penalties for offences.

Tswana 60   A wife is judged by her husband.=

Tswana 61   A hut is judged by its owner.(= If a wife commits adultery or runs away with another man, or a daughter is made pregnant, the husband or father is entitled to claim damages from her seducer and to specify the amount).

Tswana 62   The owner decides about fields.(= If cattle enter a field and injure the standing crops, the owner of the field fixes the amount of compensation due).

According to Schapera, there is a universally recognized form of penalty for other offences. "In the old days, for example, homicide was punished by death; similarly, in assault cases, the *lex talionis* was often applied, the victim being ordered to inflict upon his assailant the same kind of injury as he himself had received":[23]

Tswana 65   A life goes out for a life /a head for a head. Tswana 66   Removal (= theft of cattle) opens the kraal at the back.(= All the thief's cattle may be taken from him).

Tswana 68   A stinking man stinks together with his possessions.(= If a wife deserts her husband she must forfeit whatever he has given her: if he is not good enough to live with, neither are his possessions good enough to be kept).

Tswana 69   If a maiden shakes her head /they (the cattle) will likewise shake their tails.(= If a woman leaves her husband, through no fault of his, he can reclaim his *bogadi* = bridewealth from her father, provided the marriage is childless).

Tswana 71   When herdboys trouble each other /they must be parted.(= When people who live together quarrel continuously, the best solution is to separate them).

Litigants as well as the chief are sometimes urged not to be too hard on

(23) Schapera, *Africa* 36, p.129,

people in court:

Tswana 73   A debt is paid on the point of a needle.=

Tswana 74   'Take this' is better than darkness.(= A little is better than nothing; take what you can get, lest you get nothing more).

Tswana 75   A village is gathered with a twig /it is not taken with a club.(= Don't be too hard on people in court).

According to Schapera, these are by no means the only proverbs used in court. The proverb has in addition a general function of admonition and warning far beyond the narrow confines of the judicial system.

What makes the proverb so useful as a carrier of legal tradition is its succinct form. "Many maxims, moreover, are couched in simple and direct language; there is nothing elusive about them, but, on the contrary, they state succinctly and to the point what the legal norm is."[24]

It has further to be born in mind that the Tswana were a non-literate people. Consequently, legal rules could only be formulated orally and, therefore, had to be brief and unambiguous. With the arrival of writing as the result of European colonialism such pithy formulations were no longer necessary, but judgments and new laws could be written down and stated in much greater detail. A similar process was operative in Israel, as is shown by the contrast between short apodictic sayings and long elaborate law codes.

An older monograph that is still worth consulting is that by the Yale Research Associate in Anthropology, George Herzog, *Jabo Proverbs from Liberia*.[25] The Jabo word for proverb literally means 'old matters'. According to Herzog, "in the Jabo conception, then, 'to take old matters' apparently means to take an old situation and apply it to the present. This is presumably the chief function of a proverb: to cope with a situation as it arises, by regarding it in the light of something that has occurred before."[26]

As in other parts of Africa, the proverb plays an important part in the legal tradition of the Jabo. After the facts of a case have been established, the chief aim of the legal system is to clarify it. "It may be adjudged on the basis of an existing law, or of precedents not yet formulated as a law. In either circumstance, as with us, the case is not judged by itself; in order to be dealt with it must cease to be a particular occurrence. In this light it is significant that this process of generalizing the particular case employs the body of formulae which performs that very function – the proverbs."[27]

(24) Schapera, *Africa* 36, p.132,

(25) *Maxims in the Life of a Native Tribe*, Oxford/London 1936 = Jabo.

(26) Herzog, *Jabo Proverbs*, p.1,

(27) Herzog, ibid.

As among the Anang of Nigeria, the spokesmen of the two sides in a Jabo court case have ample opportunity for argument. Therefore, parables and proverbs are an important part of their armoury. "The more proverbs a man has at his command and the better he knows how to apply them, the better lawyer or spokesman he is considered to be. A proverb misquoted or applied badly may spoil the entire case."[28]

P. Doll[29] had argued that the function of the Creation of Man in the proverbs concerning rich and poor is to resolve social conflict. This is also the case in Jabo proverbs: "Another important function of the proverbs is to smooth social friction and dissatisfaction, and to ease the individual in his efforts to adjust himself in his setting and fate."[30] Doll attributed such sayings to socially responsible elders.[31] A corresponding observation is made by Herzog among the Jabo of Liberia: "The proverb is usually quoted to the disturbed individual by a senior, and it comes as the voice of the ancestors, his seniors *par excellence*."[32] This confirms my argument against Doll that such social criticism has its setting in the life of a tribal society - in Israel in the period of the Judges - and that its use during the monarchy is a case of re-application (Doll: *Neuinterpretation*).

Herzog gives three examples of Jabo proverbs relating to the judicial system:

Jabo 222   A lie in court saves the case. (= The implication is that a little argument may save the case or at least lessen the defeat. The legal implications of the proverb are better appreciated if one bears in mind that, as a rule, a crime is not considered to be proved, nor is the culprit fully convicted, unless a confession has been made). - The same is true in early Israel, cf. Achan's theft and his sacral confession, Josh.7.1-26.[33]

Jabo 339   One does not settle a court case by messenger.

Jabo 356   Sending a mannerless person into the intertribal court / defeats the case of the nation. (= The proverb applies to any situation in which trouble and loss are caused by placing the wrong person in charge of a matter he could not have been

(28) Herzog, *Jabo Proverbs*, p.2,

(29) P. Doll, *Menschenschöpfung und Weltschöpfung in der alttestamentlichen Weisheit*, Stuttgart 1985, p.29,

(30) Herzog, ibid.

(31) Doll, *Menschenschöpfung*, p.26,

(32) Herzog, *Jabo Proverbs*, p.2,

(33) F. Horst, "Die Doxologien im Amos-Buch", *ZAW* 47, 1929, pp.45-54, and J.L. Crenshaw, "The Influence of the Wise upon Amos", *ZAW* 79, 1967, pp.42-52.

expected to handle satisfactorily).

While the legal proverbs of the Anang, Tswana, and Jabo have been investigated in detail, these proverbs are, nevertheless, widespread among all peoples of Africa:

The Malagasy of Madagascar[34] have a large number of such proverbs:

Mal.927	Persecutors of the weak /will be persecuted by the strong.
Mal.1060	No thief is so blamable as the stealer of money.
Mal.1065	Dance in a stolen jacket /and dance with distress.
Mal.1066	Stealing kills / but begging keeps alive.
Mal.1068	Don't do like Ima'haka':steal a sheep by pretending to try its weight.
Mal.1071	Like a dog with a black mouth /he looks as if he has stolen the food.
Mal.1074	Not bald, not wounded /yet he keeps covering his head.(= suspicious circumstance).
Mal.1077	Robbers fighting in the desert /those who conquer tell the sovereign.(= of the wicked men who attacked them).
Mal.1079	They are both guilty /for one is the little basket / that took it out /and the other the big basket / that took it away.
Mal.1083	Love law / and lose money. (= litigation).
Mal.1084	Let it be talk /for if it is going to be law /the property is wasted.
Mal.1085	A long suit / and poor recompense.
Mal.1089	Did you think I should be lost /that you forsook me at the trial?
Mal.1091	Don't let a sleeper's robe /be taken by the one who wakes (first). (= unfair advantage).
Mal.1092	Don't kill me when upright / like a tree.(= innocent person).
Mal.1093	Cut me / but don't cut me with the edge /cut with the back. (= mild punishment).
Mal.1096	A dog that has stolen the sheep / his life is forfeit.(= Referring to those guilty of capital offences).
Mal.1189	Don't weigh with false scales! - a common biblical injunction.[35]

(34) J.A. Houlder, *OHABOLANA or Malagasy Proverbs I & II*, Antananarivo 1915/16 (= Mal.),

(35) Cf.Amos 8.5; Hos.12.8; Mic.6.11; Prov.11.1; 20.23.

About 5% of the Tonga proverbs[36] deal with law, crime, and justice:

Ton.29   Deceitful crocodile / who seizes even the calabashes (tied to the poles for drawing water).(= Said of somebody who comes with flattering words to you, but who is out for robbery and trouble).

Ton.47   Nobody dares to dig open a mamba's hole /but everybody dares to look into it.(= When a cunning or aggressive person has done something wrong, it is right to question him, even if he tries to stop the process).

Ton.63   The duiker which frequently goes in the fields /is often caught.(= A man who habitually steals will eventually be caught and fined).

Ton.76   (= Bantu[37] p.47) They have beaten the bush /they have not beaten the hare.(= They have missed the culprit in the matter, though they have searched for him).

Ton.115   The snail leaves its foam wherever it goes.(= The one who does wrong does not know that others see him. Therefore he tries to deny his guilt).

Ton.117   The tortoise has struck a log.(= Do not proceed with a case when it has proved too much for you).

Ton.145 (= Bantu p.48) A goat suffering from scab /rubs itself against the poles of the kraal.(= A person who has stolen or committed some other offence usually defends himself by accusing others).

Ton.161   When a dog cannot bark /it has a bone in the mouth.(= When a man cannot reprove another for his sins, it is because he has sinned in the same way).

Ton.191   You have made me: 'Little cock, go to sleep!'(= I have been deceived, cheated by one who appeared to be a good man).

Ton.211   The quail has set itself free to escape.(= The accused has obtained freedom by defending himself).

Ton.264   The chief has no relative. (= he is impartial). Ton.280 A solitary man is not listened to (in court) /because he has no witnesses. Ton.379 People soften a skin in court.(= While a matter is discussed in court people break the ties which bind them to each other). Ton.385 One pulls out a thorn

(36) H.P. Junod and A.A. Jaques, *The Wisdom of the Tonga-Shangaan People*, Cleveland/ Transvaal 1936 (= Ton.),

(37) H.P. Junod, *Bantu Heritage*, Johannesburg 1938, pp.46ff (= Bantu),

the way it got in.(= To discuss a case one must begin at the beginning). Ton.386 He who prays for mercy is not killed /it is the fierce fighter who is killed.(= A fine or punishment is not imposed upon the one who asks for forgiveness, but the one who defends himself by pleading not guilty suffers punishment). Ton.392 Beat the winnowing-basket /(the fools will be surprised).(= In a court case, when you are in difficulties, do something, act in a queer fashion. The people present may be surprised, and you may escape).

Ton.396   He left his leg outside.(= He is not giving a full account of the matter. He only wants to delay it).

Ton.399   The sore on the nose is not shown.(= Though a man may deny his guilt when he is obviously guilty, the matter is quite clear. He defends himself in vain).

Ton.403   They did not find the way to cut (the meat).(= They failed to find a way of settling a matter).

Ton.405   A case does not rot.(= When a matter has been brought to light it will not vanish until it has been properly settled). Ton.413 To sleep with an ember on the sore.(= The settlement of a case, it is painful).

Ton.424   A person who is innocent /will be defended by many people.(= If you are innocent, you will be found not guilty by the majority of the court). Ton.435 So and So has one finger. (= is a robber). Ton.439 The ball has struck the knee.(= Said when a man denies his guilt, and witnesses called prove that he is really guilty of the crime he denies).

Ton.564   The hoes clash together.(= When the cattle of a man or his people kill each other, there is no case).

Ton.613   One does not find water by grating a stone.(= It does not help to begin a case, if you do not know how to proceed). Ton.844 It is an eel.(= Said of a man who is in the habit of stealing and cannot be caught. He glides like a fish).

Ton.848   One does not warm oneself at the thief's fire.(= Do not make friends with thieves!). Ton.851 Do not steal / your portion will come.(= Though you may be hungry, refrain from stealing, you will have your share later on).

The following is a small selection of the proverbs of the Kundu of Cameroon[38] dealing with law, crime, and justice:

(38) J. Ittmann, *Sprichwörter der Kundu*, Berlin 1971 (= Kundu),

Kundu 330   The porcupine nearby is not in a habit of eating the nuts.(= A thief normally does not belong to the same village). Kundu 711 The polecat has died with the fruit in its cheek.(= The thief has been caught red-handed).

Kundu 832   A goat pointed to with one's fingers /easily gives birth to twins.(= If someone has a reputation for being a thief and something of this kind happens, he is immediately under suspicion).

Kundu 694   Even if you are plagued by hunger /do not go out stealing. Kundu 718 A free man does not steal.

Kundu 841   The stomach brings about the death of the head.(= Someone has stolen, because he was hungry, and now he is being punished as a thief). Kundu 167 If the elephant wants to kill someone /he goes with him to the stem of a tree (in order to squash him).(= If the judge has recognized all the evidence for the guilt of the defendant, he sums up all the reasons for convicting him). Kundu 795 Chasing many debts in court leads to poverty.(= The creditor loses his possessions ..., because, according to African law, he has to pay costs, even when he wins). Kundu 423 A banana plant not fully grown has no ripe fruits.(= A case has to be well discussed in order to come to a solution).

Kundu 982   A mouth cannot pronounce judgment.(= does not have the strength to enforce it).Kundu 1301 Without knowing a strange settlement /you intend to dream about it?(= You cannot appear as a witness in a matter of which you have no knowledge).

Legal proverbs occur also elsewhere:

Fante[39] p.512 It takes time to make a dress for the hunchback.(= Request for the postponement of a case).

Fante p.513 Some must inform the sea to stop being rough /so that the coconut branches may stop rustling.(= Order in court!). Lov.[40]

p.193 A dog which eats another cannot grow fat.(= A murderer must always be killed). Kaf.[41]

(39) J.B. Christensen, "The Role of Proverbs in Fante Culture", in E.P. Skinner (ed.), *Peoples and Cultures of Africa*, New York 1973, pp.509ff (= Fante).

(40) E.J. and J.D. Krige, The *Realm of a Rain-Queen*, London 1943 (= Lov.),

(41) G. McCall, *Kaffir Folk-lore*, 1892 (= Kaf.),

p.185 The shield turned the wrong way.(= One who turns evidence against accomplices in a crime). Kaf.(2)[42]

p.295 Let the bottle of the ear be filled!(= Tell all; make a full confession). Kam.[43]

44 If something moves off in the dry season /it is returned by the rains.(= This saw is often used of a person who has committed a crime, and for that reason been obliged to flee his village. When the affair has blown over he will return).- Cf. Rebecca's advice to Jacob, Gen.27.42-45. Aki.[44] p.216 What is in one's heart is no evidence.(ibid) A tribunal never jumps over a stream.(= Justice must not be hurried). Aki. p.217 Being caught is not being imprisoned.(= The judgment is left).

Nandi 18[45] A tree is not twice struck by lightning.(= If you have to punish a person or tribe, do it so thoroughly that it will not require to be done a second time). Nandi 51 If a dead tree falls /it carries with it a live one.(= If a criminal is punished, his innocent relations suffer as well). Ovim.[46]

p.254 You cannot tie a buck's head in a cloth /the horns will stick out.(= Crime cannot be concealed, murder will out).

Ewe[47] 70 The part of the stick that is in the fire will be burned.(= Punishment only falls on the guilty). Hausa[48] 37 You condemn on hear-say evidence alone /your sins increase.

Having surveyed a large number of African proverbs relating to law, crime, and justice and cases of proverb performance among the Anang, Tswana, and Jabo, let us now return to the Old Testament. The Hebrew prophets, too, refer to justice in the gate (cf. Amos 5.10,12,15) and we hear of cases that were discussed in the gate (Gen.23.10,18; Job 29.7; Prov.24.7; 31.23). "In every town disputes and trials were settled by the Elders, that is, the heads of families in the clan, the leading citizens of the place."[49]

(42) Dudley Kidd, *The Essential Kafir*, London 1904 (= Kaf.2),

(43) G. Lindblom, *Kamba Folklore III*, Uppsala 1934, pp.28ff (= Kam.),

(44) C. Cagnolo, *The Akikuyu. The Customs, Traditions and Folklore*, Nyeri/Kenia 1933, pp.214ff (= Aki.),

(45) A.C. Hollis, *The Nandi. Their Language and Folklore*, Oxford 1909 = 1969 (= Nandi),

(46) W.D. Hamby, *The Ovimbundu of Angola*, Chicago 1934 (= Ovim.),

(47) A.B. Ellis, *The EWE-Speaking Peoples*, London 1890 (= Ewe),

(48) R.S. Rattray, *Hausa Folk-lore II*, Oxford 1913, pp.254ff (= Hausa),

(49) R. de Vaux, *Ancient Israel. Its Life and Institutions*, London 2 1965, p.152; on court procedure cf. pp.155-57.

It would, therefore, appear that the judicial system of tribal societies in Africa and Israel is very much alike. The cases of proverb performance and the legal proverbs of Africa provide therefore the *necessary condition* for Gerstenberger's claim (see above) that Israel's apodictic law has its origin in clan wisdom – the clan wisdom of sedentary farmers. The *sufficient condition* for such an argument can, however, only be established from the Old Testament itself. The paucity of clearly identifiable material makes this difficult, if not impossible. The reason for this is the relatively early introduction of writing in Israel. Once it has become possible to transmit legal norms in writing, the use of legal proverbs is somewhat pointless – as the recent Tswana example from Bechuanaland clearly shows – because written transmission is generally regarded as safer.

6

Family and Kinship

This topic is important both for the student of the Old Testament and the social anthropologist. The biblical proverbs show clearly that education was the task of the family and not that of schools.[1] In social anthropology the classificatory system of family and kinship provides the key to our understanding of *La Pensée Sauvage* (Lévi-Strauss), primitive man's view of himself and his world.[2]

Just under four dozen biblical proverbs and exhortations in Prov.10-29

(1) R. de Vaux, *Ancient Israel. Its Life and Institutions*, 2, 1965, pp.19-61; Joh.s Pedersen, *Israel. Its Life and Culture I-II*, London/Copenhagen 1926, pp.46-96,

(2) The best introduction to the anthropological discussion is provided by Robin Fox, *Kinship and Marriage. An anthropological Perspective*, Penguin, Harmondsworth, Middlesex 1967. For Africa cf. the collection ed. by A.R. Radcliffe-Brown and D. Forde, *African Systems of Kinship and Marriage*, Oxford 1950, and here esp. the Introduction by Radcliffe-Brown, pp.1-85, and the essays by M. Fortes, pp.252-84, D. Forde, pp.285-332, and E.E. Evans-Pritchard, pp.360-91, dealing with matrilineal (Ashanti), double (Yak), and patrilineal descent (Nuer) respectively. These introductory books are based on detailed anthropological field work, e.g. by Sir Edward E. Evans-Pritchard, *The Nuer. A Description of the Modes of Livelihood and Political Institutions of a Nilotic People*, Oxford 1968 = 1940, and *Kinship and Marriage among the Nuer*, Oxford 1966 = 1951. The Nuer are of special interest to Old Testament scholars, because, like Israel during the period of the Judges, they are a people consisting of tribes without permanent rulers. Similarly useful studies are: Esther N. Goody, *Contexts of Kinship. An Essay in the Family Sociology of the Gonja in Northern Ghana*, Cambridge 1973, and the collection of essays ed. by John L. Comaroff, *The Meaning of Marriage Payments*, London et al. 1980. For a more abstract discussion of the problem of family and kinship cf. C. Lévi-Strauss, *The Elementary Structures of Kinship*, London 1969, and Luc de Heusch, *Why Marry Her? Society and Symbolic Structures*, Cambridge 1981. De Heusch defends Lévi-Strauss's ideas with results derived from field work done in Zaire, the former Belgian Congo.- I wish to thank Dr. Wendy James of the Oxford University Institute of Social and Cultural Anthropology for her helpful advice regarding anthropological literature.

(3) *Ancient Israel*, pp.48f,

and the poem about the good housewife, Prov.31.10-31, deal with family and kinship. This includes a dozen sayings on education, because, according to de Vaux, "during his early years a child was left to the care of his mother or nurse, even after he had been weaned (II Sam.4.4) and was learning to walk (Hos.11.3). The little Israelite spent most of his time playing in the streets or squares with boys and girls of his own age.... It was the mother who gave her children the first rudiments of education, especially of their moral formation (Prov.1.8; 6.20). She might continue to advise her children even in adolescence (Prov.31.1), but as the boys grew up to manhood, they were usually entrusted to their father."[3]

Prov.12.1   Whoever loves discipline loves knowledge /but he who hates reproof is stupid. Prov.13.1 A wise son hears his father's instruction /but a scoffer does not listen to rebuke.

Rejecting instruction can lead to poverty:

Prov.13.18   Poverty and disgrace come to him who ignores instruction /but he who heeds reproof is honoured. Prov.15.5 A fool despises his father's instruction /but he who heeds admonition is prudent.

Prov.15.10   There is severe discipline for him who forsakes the way / he who hates reproof will die.

Prov.15.32   He who ignores instruction despises himself /but he who heeds admonition gains understanding.

Similar advice is given in the collection based on Amen-em-ope:

Prov.23.22   Hearken to your father who begot you /and do not despise your mother when she is old.

Whip and rod were obviously used in education:[4]

Prov.13.24   He who spares the rod hates his son /but he who loves him is diligent to discipline him. Prov.20.30 Blows that wound cleanse away evil /strokes make clean the innermost parts.

Similarly under the influence of Amen-em-ope:

Prov.23.13+14 Do not withhold discipline from a child /if you beat him with a rod, he will not die. If you beat him with the rod /you will save his life from Sheol.

Prov.29.15   The rod and reproof give wisdom /but a child left to himself brings shame to his mother. Prov.29.17 Discipline your son, and he will give you rest /he will give delight to your heart.

(4) Cf. de Vaux, *Ancient Israel*, p.49,
(5) Lévi-Strauss, *Elementary Structures*, p.135,

But corporal punishment is not to be overdone:

Prov.19.18   Discipline your son while there is hope /do not set your
             heart on his destruction.

Together with education we can consider a group of family proverbs
which overlap with 'Wisdom and Folly':

Prov.10.1   A wise son makes a glad father /but a foolish son is a sorrow
            to his mother.

The combination of the pair 'wise/foolish' with 'father/mother' can also
be found in

Prov.15.20   A wise son makes a glad father /but a foolish man despises
             his mother, and in Prov.17.25 A foolish son is grief to his
             father /and the bitterness of her who bore him.

Prov.10.5   A son who gathers in the summer is prudent /but a son who
            sleeps in the harvest brings shame.

Prov.28.7   He who keeps the law is a wise son /but a companion of
            gluttons shames his father. Prov.29.3 He who loves wisdom
            makes his father glad /but one who keeps company with
            harlots squanders his substance.

Tough luck, if you are smitten both with a foolish son and a contentious
wife:

Prov.19.13   A foolish son is ruin to his father /and a wife's quarrelling
             is a continual dripping of rain.

The contentious woman is obviously a very widespread phenomenon:

Prov.21.9 = 25.24 It is better to live in a corner of the housetop /than
                  in a house shared with a contentious woman.
                  Prov.21.19 It is better to live in a desert land /than
                  with a contentious and fretful woman.

The image of the continual dripping of rain from Prov.19.13 is taken up
again in

Prov.27.15+16: A continual dripping on a rainy day /and a contentious
                woman are alike /to restrain her is to restrain the wind
                /or to grasp oil in his right hand.

Being aware of the dangers of taking a bad wife, the proverbialist also
sings the praises of the good one (cf. the poem Prov.31.10-31):

Prov.12.4   A good wife is the crown of her husband /but she who
            brings shame is like rottenness in his bones.

Prov.18.22 He who finds a wife finds a good thing /and obtains favour
            from the LORD. Prov.19.14 House and wealth are
            inherited from the fathers /but a prudent wife is from the
            LORD.

In tribal Israel as in other primitive societies bachelorhood is generally pitied or looked down upon: "The 'poor and desperate' bachelor (Frazer) who cannot obtain a wife in the normal manner by exchange is forced to lead the life of an outlaw, for his only chance lies in carrying off one of the women of his group, or in capturing a woman from another group. In both cases, however, the group will turn against him, either out of solidarity with the injured member, or through fear of trouble with other groups."[5]

There are two general observations on women, whether married or single:

Prov.11.16   A gracious woman gets honour /and 'active' men get riches.[6] Prov.11.22 Like a gold ring in a swine's snout /is a beautiful woman without discretion.

Three sayings relate to parents:

Prov.19.26   He who does violence to his father and chases away his mother /is a son who causes shame and brings reproach. Prov.20.20 If one curses his father or his mother /his lamp will be put out in utter darkness. Prov.28.24 He who robs his father or his mother /and says, "That is no transgression", /is the companion of a man who destroys.

Fathers' righteousness is also a blessing to their sons: Prov.20.7 A righteous man who walks in his integrity /blessed are his sons after him. One proverb deals with the child: Prov.20.11 Even a child makes himself known by his acts /whether what he does is pure and right. Old and young are contrasted in three proverbs: Prov.17.6 Grandchildren are the crown of the aged /and the glory of sons is their fathers. Prov.20.29 The glory of young men is their strength /but the beauty of old men is their grey hair. And perhaps also Prov.16.31: A hoary head is a crown of honour /it is gained in a righteous life.

Prov.17.2 deals with the relationship of a slave to the son and heir: A slave who deals wisely will rule over a son who acts shamefully / and will share the inheritance as one of the brothers.

Evans-Pritchard describes how Dinka, captured by the Nuer as slaves, are eventually incorporated into Nuer lineages: "Captured Dinka boys are almost invariably incorporated in the lineage of their Nuer captors by the rite of adoption, and then they rank as sons in lineage structure as well as in family relations, and when the daughters of that lineage are married they receive bride-cattle. A Dinka boy is brought up as a child of his captor's

(6) Plöger, BK XVII, ad loc.
(7) Evans-Pritchard, *The Nuer*, pp.221f,

household. He is already incorporated into the family and the joint family by his acceptance as a member of these groups by their other members and by outsiders. People say ...'he has become a member of the community', and they say of the man who captured him that 'he has become his father', and of his sons that 'they have become his brothers'. He is already a member of the *gol*, the household and joint family. Adoption gives him a position in the lineage structure, and thereby ceremonial status, for by adoption he becomes a member of his captor's *thok dwiel*, lineage."[7]

Inheritance is also the subject of Prov.20.21 An inheritance gotten hastily in the beginning /will in the end not be blessed.

Two proverbs deal with kinship solidarity:

Prov.17.17　A friend loves at all times /and a brother (= kinsman) is born for adversity. Prov.18.19 A brother (= kinsman) 'deceived is stronger than' a fortified city /but quarrelling is like the bars of a castle.[8]

In tribal societies people only travel a few miles from home for fear of lack of protection:

Prov.27.8　Like a bird that strays from its nest /is a man who strays from his home.

John T. Milimo has investigated the proverbs of his own people, the Plateau Tonga of Zambia, and devoted a section of his thesis to family and kinship.[9] According to Milimo,[10] the Tonga proverbs show an exceedingly low opinion of women:

Tonga 150　Who listens to women /suffered from famine at harvest time.

While this may also be the case in the biblical proverbs concerning the contentious woman (Prov.21.9,19; 25.24; 27.15+16), these are balanced by others praising the good wife (Prov.12.4; 18.22; 19.14; 31.10-31).

The Tonga seem to think that women can be taken and divorced as often as one wishes:

Tonga 134　One may have no clansmen /but one will never lack a woman to marry.

The Nuer by contrast try to prevent divorce at all cost in order to avoid having to return bridewealth: "Divorce is due to failure of one or other of the parties to live up to the code of conduct expected of him or her, and

(8) Plöger, BK XVII, ad loc.
(9) J.T. Milimo, *A Study of the Proverbial Lore of the Plateau Tonga of Zambia*, B.Litt. thesis, Oxford 1976, esp. pp.122-29 (= Tonga).
(10) Milimo, *Tonga*, p.122,

Nuer regard it as a misfortune in which there is also an element of the shameful."[11] This is closer to the biblical attitude.

However, according to Milimo, "women's role in a man's life is acknowledged. They, together with their children, are the ones who build up men's names and fame"[12]: Tonga 142 The richness of the roof is the wall. Tonga 143 The weight of a hen is its feathers.

Like most African peoples, the Plateau Tonga favour cross cousin marriage: Tonga 138 A child returns to the womb (= the bride comes back to the clan of the speaker).

The nest-dweller attitude of Prov.27.8 is shared by Tonga 141 The bride (groom) does not go across a stream.

By taking a wife one has also got to take care of her relatives: Tonga 158+159 Who plucks the pumpkin take also the plant.

In a polygamous marriage among the Plateau Tonga the first wife is honoured above the others:[13] Tonga 144 It is the first one that makes the home.

Children are the responsibility of every adult member of the community:[14] Tonga 155 A child is begotten by the community.

A mother cares for her children before thinking of herself: Tonga 156 A mother-mouse does not make her own stomach sweet.

Children often resemble their parents who might be already dead:[15] Tonga 145 The legs of the deceased are recognized in his offspring.

Attitudes similar to those enshrined in the biblical proverbs seem to have been observed by Herzog among the Jabo of Liberia.[16] "The individual can make himself effective only through the channels which his culture offers him. Thus the value placed on solidarity and co-operation, and the prizing of the home."[17] For the former cf. Prov.17.17; 18.19 and for the latter Prov.27.8. "In relations between individuals, seniority is one of the most powerful factors; hence numerous examples which expose the relation to each other of age, experience, accomplishment, and responsibility."[18] Cf. Prov.16.31; 17.6; 20.29. "It is through this relation that the individual acquires his right to his share of social goods" - cf. Prov.17.17; 18.19 -. "But

(11) Evans-Pritchard, *Kinship and Marriage among the Nuer*, p.96,

(12) Milimo, *Tonga*, p.125,

(13) Milimo, ibid.

(14) Milimo, *Tonga*, p.126,

(15) Milimo, *Tonga*, p.128,

(16) G. Herzog, *Jabo Proverbs from Liberia*, Oxford 1936,

(17) Herzog, *Jabo*, p.6,

(18) Herzog, ibid.

the enjoyment of these is also dependent upon his regard for the appropriate means, proper procedure, and social sanction":[19]

a) Solidarity and co-operation

Jabo 23   One cannot fight on two roads.(= If Upper Nimiah and Lower Nimiah both join in a decision, it will be easy to carry out. But if they make independent efforts, it would be like fighting on two roads at the same time).

Jabo 69   Termite says: The burden of the multitude is not heavy. Jabo 195 If the house-post breaks /the whole house falls to the ground. Jabo 204 If we form a bundle /we cannot be broken. Jabo 205 Paddle advises paddle. Jabo 259 Where relatives gather /there is confidence. Jabo 260 When your relative dies /it is you who shave your head.- Cf. Job 1.20. Jabo 263 If you have nobody /you perish an orphan.

b) Home

Jabo 193   A man who has no house /is like a bird in the tree when a storm has broken. Jabo 322 The house-father is respected at his own hearth.(= A man is always treated with respect and consideration in his home or in his town). Jabo 362 One who roams the land does not witness his father's burial.(= Not only does the roamer miss the burial of his father, he also misses the subsequent settlement of the property. The proverb is used when a person by his absence or careless behaviour loses important opportunities).

c) Age, experience, responsibility

Jabo 31   A tree grows up /before we tie a cow to it.(= Experience and standing are necessary before one can achieve the position that will make others place their trust in him). Jabo 36 It is the full-grown forest that yields the buffalo. Jabo 46 The palm-nuts ripen /before the birds will nibble at them. Jabo 77 Catfish says: Your skull hardens /before you swim upstream. Jabo 141 After she is grown /the cow breaks the hills. Jabo 293 If you have no child /you will not give advice about children. Jabo 321 It is the house-father /who gives

(19) Herzog, ibid.

largely.(= The lord and not the servant is the one who is expected to act generously, and for whom it is proper).

d) Share of social goods

Jabo 245 If you don't go to war /you don't eat of the war-cow.(= One cannot receive a reward without having taken the risks and done the share expected of him). Jabo 296 The child on the mother's back /does not see the fish in the water.(= The right to decide belongs to me).Similarly: Jabo 297 The child does not cut the wing of his father's chicken. Jabo 298 A child this small does not go /where the war-medicine-dog is butchered.(= Dogs are eaten chiefly to effect war-magic, a feast of which a child is not permitted to partake).

e) Proper procedure and social sanction

Jabo 7 A spirit does not take just anything /it takes ivory.(= praising a dead person). Jabo 198 If one goes to farm /he takes not a knife but a cutlass.(= The proverb is applied when the procedure selected is not the proper one or when the means employed are not sufficient to bring about the desired end). Jabo 299 A child does not speak when a grown-up is talking.

Jabo proverbs like biblical ones are used "for minimizing friction and effecting adjustment .... Far from being dead clichés which proverbs are for us, they form a vital and potent element of the culture they interpret."[20]

Before looking at African attitudes to kinship as expressed in proverbs, we need to consider the political and social background of such sayings. On the strength of his field work among the Nuer, Evans-Pritchard advises a threefold distinction between:

"(1) *political distance* in the sense of structural distance between segments of a tribe, the largest political unit, and between tribes in a system of political relations; (2) *general structural distance* in the sense of non-political distance between various social groups in the Nuer-speaking community - non-political structural relations are strongest between adjacent tribes, but a common social structure embraces the whole of Nuerland; and (3) *the social sphere of an individual*, being his circuit of social contacts of one kind or

(20) Herzog, *Jabo*, p.15,

another with other Nuer."[21] This distinction holds good for other African tribal societies and would probably not have been alien to tribal Israel either.

According to Evans-Pritchard, a tribe has been traditionally defined by (1) a common and distinct name; (2) a common sentiment; (3) a common and distinct territory; (4) a moral obligation to unite in war; and (5) a moral obligation to settle feuds and other disputes by arbitration. To these five points Evans-Pritchard adds "three further characteristics...: (6) a tribe is a segmented structure and there is opposition between its segments; (7) within each tribe there is a dominant clan and the relation between the lineage structure of this clan and the territorial system of the tribe is of great structural importance; (8) a tribe is a unit in a system of tribes; and (9) age-sets are organized tribally."[22] Points 1-8 would have applied to the Israel of the period of the Judges, about (9) we have no information.

That there should be parallels between the Nuer and tribal Israel is not really surprising, because both peoples consist of tribes without rulers.[23] What Evans-Pritchard observed among the Nuer, the lack of governmental organs, the absence of legal institutions, of developed leadership, and of organized political life could equally be said of Israel during the period of the Judges. Her legal cases were settled on an *ad hoc* basis in the town gate, and her charismatic leaders went back to the plough after having liberated their tribe and its neighbours. And the following statement about the Nuer might well have been written about early Israel: "The ordered anarchy in which they live accords well with their character, for it is impossible to live among Nuer and conceive of rulers ruling over them."[24] Ancient Israel only changed her mind when confronted by the Philistine threat.

And the following description of Nuer character also sounds strangely familiar to the reader of the Old Testament: "The Nuer is a product of hard and egalitarian upbringing, is deeply democratic, and easily roused to violence. His turbulent spirit finds any restraint irksome and no man recognizes a superior. Wealth makes no difference. A man with many cattle is envied, but not treated differently from a man with few cattle. Birth makes no difference. A man may not be a member of the dominant clan of his tribe, he may even be of Dinka descent, but were another to allude to the fact he would run a grave risk of being clubbed."[25]

(21) Evans-Pritchard, *The Nuer*, pp.124f,

(22) Evans-Pritchard, *The Nuer*, p.122,

(23) J. Middleton and D. Tait (ed.s), *Tribes Without Rulers. Studies in African Segmentary Systems*, London 1958,

(24) Evans-Pritchard, *The Nuer*, p.181,

(25) Evans-Pritchard, ibid.

The following are African proverbs relating to

a) Kinship.

Mal.218 Don't do wrong to a friend or relative /for you won't get another.

Mal.229 The side of a stone is a stone /the side of wood is wood / the side of a relative (i.e. a distant relative) is a relative.

Mal.252 They who are one as regards children are one in chat.

Mal.745 He likes to do good /and therefore does so to his nearest relatives.

Mal.1888 Don't be sorrowful for your own child only. Mal.1899 A brother is like the bottom of the cattle pen: /good or bad, whatever happens is told to him (by the sister).(= Most Malagasy women think that a brother is far more to be confided in than their husband). Ton.25 The strength of the crocodile is in the water.(= A man is helpless without his own kin). Ton.82 They beat each other with a baboon's bone.(= They help each other because they are relatives).

Two proverbs state that domestic quarrels are unavoidable:

Ton.128 Oxen fight each other in the kraal; and Ton.129 Sono's cattle play with each other with their horns. Ton.159 A wet dog has no master.(= If a member of your family has done something wrong, you do not wish to admit that he is one of your kin). Ton.179 A daughter is a hen /to be caught for the people passing by.(= When a daughter marries she leaves the village and goes away). Ton.181 A hen boasts of its breed.(= Everybody is proud of his own people and boasts that they are superior to others).Similar to Ton.25 is Ton.222: Do not take fish out of the water / it will die.(= Do not separate a person from his relatives!). Ton.269 People are wealth.(= The real wealth of a man is his kith and kin). Ton.466 The *nkanye* tree which is on the boundary has no owner.(= A son belongs to all who are his relatives. They will all send him on errands and use his services, although they may not be on good terms among themselves). Ton.508 People swallow a medicine /when they know it.(= People marry through kith and kin. One does not take as a wife a woman one does not know). Ton.516 A man polishes his own spear.(= A man must look after his own village and family = Charity begins at home). Ton.541 The ties established between two families by a happy marriage /are stronger than those of money. Ton.542 The family-in-law is the hip of the elephant.(= something very big). Ton.543 The friends of a person may clean up his vomit /but his brothers will clean up his blood. Ton.548 Houses built close together burn together.(= People who live close to each other should help each other). Ton.549 One leg does not dance alone.(= A solitary person does not get any fun out of life).Ton.552 A relative by marriage /is the little knife on one's hip.(= A relative by marriage has given one one's wife. One can have confidence in him and rely on his help). Ton.555 The place where your people are /is not far away. Ton.558 Wealth is bits of roasted meat /the great thing is one's kith and kin. Ton.560 To see each other is to go on.(= Nobody is ever tired of seeing the ones he loves, especially his home people). Fante p.514 The lizard and the crocodile have the same stomach /if one eats / the other should also get a morsel.(= being of the same clan). ibid. The poor kinsman does not lack a resting place. ibid. If you are getting your hair cut by your mother's child /you do not look into the looking glass.(= Kinsmen are to be trusted). ibid. Because the tortoise has no clan /he has already made his casket. ibid. The right arm washed the left arm /and the left also washed the right. ibid. A bird roosts with his own clan. ibid. The good paw paw tree has a plucking stick near it.(= The wealthy man will have less fortunate kinsmen around him). Fante p.515 One does not show which thigh the day will find one sleeping on.(= It is believed to be unwise to show a high degree of favouritism to a specific sister's son). Bantu p.48 Partridges' kith and kin scratch the ground together. Kaf. p.185 You are lighting a fire in the wind.(= Anyone who favours strangers in preference or to the loss of relatives). Lunda p.282 To fall out with the ford /there are deep pools.(= To fall out with one's relatives is trouble).

The following group of proverbs deals with

b) Marriage / divorce

Esther N. Goody describes the process of marriage among the Gonja of Northern Ghana as follows:

"(1) Courtship always means courting gifts and the gradual establishment of a relationship ... between the man and the woman. An arranged marriage tends to be either the consequence of a similar pattern of greeting and gift-giving from the husband to the bride's kin, or else an expression of gift-giving and respectful deference by the bride's kin to the groom. (2) The involvement of the families of bride and groom is expressed in the sending and accepting of the marriage kola. The bride must at least appear to agree before the kola are accepted. (3) At her first marriage a girl ought to display reluctance to leave her family. (4) Removal of the bride to the groom's compound is followed by her seclusion for a period of time. (5) In one or more different ways the bride is introduced to the household and community of her husband. (6) In one or more different ways the bride is established as a wife with rights to domestic facilities, farm land, and to her husband's attentions over and against other wives."[26]

For the Malagasy the stability of marriage and the family rests on a harmonious wedded life and love between the partners (cf. Mal.1744 + 1745). Evans-Pritchard is also prepared to admit "that the stability of Nuer marriage rests on quite other foundations than the payments of bridewealth: affection between the spouses, the good reputation of the husband, mutual good will between the families of husband and wife, especially personal friendship between the fathers or between the husband and his wife's brother, and moral and legal norms."[27]

Marriage is only fully consummated when the first child has been born. "Nuer have good grounds for their assumption that a newly-wed who has borne her husband a child and brought it to his hearth is satisfied with her mate. By the time a second child is born experience has shown that the pair are agreeable to one another also as domestic partners. As Nuer observe a weaning taboo, this means at least three years after the birth of the first child."[28] Hence the importance of a large number of children to the African family.

> Mal.1739   Marriage is for companionship /child-bearing for heirship.
> Mal.1741 A forced marriage is unendurable. Similarly
> Mal.1742: A forced marriage means nothing but weeping.

(26) E.N. Goody, *Contexts of Kinship*, p.100,
(27) Evans-Pritchard, *Kinship*, p.95,
(28) Evans-Pritchard, ibid.

By contrast: Mal.1744 There is nothing better than a harmonious wedded life. And Mal.1745 There is no happiness /like marrying for love. Mal.1749 The lass just married has lost her wits /and gone to catch locusts in the evening.(= when they are extremely difficult to catch). Mal.1750 Would it were still as on my wedding day: /the meat was plentiful /the love was becoming stronger /and I was doubly honoured. Mal.1811 An elder daughter won't consent to have her younger sister as a rival /but the younger one consents (to become second wife to her sister's husband). - cf. Gen.29.26. Mal.1813 In a hurry to wed / in haste to part. Mal.1817 Let matrimony be like a fowl's clothing /not parted with until death.

Mal.1819 has the form of a riddle:

Miserable when added to /like a man's wife.

Mal.1832   Seven children won't hold a husband /but plenty of wisdom will. Mal.1833 To divorce a young wife /and give a blessing to others.- Similarly Mal.1839 A little one overtaken by trouble /like a man who divorced his wife in anger. Mal.1845 There are many to marry /but none to be parents in law.(= for great care is necessary in choosing them). Ton.144 When the goat gives birth to one kid only /the owner is not pleased.(= A man who wishes to become head of a big family takes many wives). Ton.170 A dog's sauce is spilt by its owner.(= The adulterous wife is left by her husband). Ton.337 If you do not travel /you will marry your sister.

The proverb presupposes the rule of exogamous marriage and the incest taboo. "The rules taken as a whole amount to this: a man must not marry kin (including affines), and as he is born and brought up in a circle of kin which normally embraces the people of his immediate neighbourhood, he is generally compelled to marry outside it."[29]

Ton. 488   God has sown plentifully /he has not sown a little).(= Those you may marry are many). Ton.489 To miss the mother's child!(= Said to ridicule a man who does not find a wife). Ton.490 The trap has caught a beast.(= The man has found a wife). Ton.493 I am not a snake /which kills and leaves its prey /I have killed to eat.(= When a young

(29) Evans-Pritchard, *Kinship*, p.35,

man has put a girl in the family way, and they ask him if he
wants to leave her, he answers with these words to show
that he did not seduce her, but wants to marry her).
Ton.494 Do not be impressed by the activity of the girl /
these good manners are only for getting married.(= Pretence
in order to find a husband). Ton.498 = Bantu p.50 Though
marriage is slow /divorce is not slow. Ton.499 To marry
with a family living nearby is not good.-There is a danger
of marrying forbidden kin. Ton.500 Marriage roasts.(= A
seed hardens when you roast it, so it is with a man's heart
in married life). Ton.501 Beautiful from behind / ugly in
front.(= One who was attractive before marriage and is
soon divorced). Ton.504 Digger of a well /others will
come only to draw water.(First the 'great' wife is married,
afterwards other wives will follow). Ton.505 = Bantu p.50
To marry is to put a snake in one's handbag. Ton.510 He
has thrown me away /like a bundle of dry wood.(= A
woman is not loved any more by her husband). Ton.513
The polygamist ploughs only one field.(= A polygamist has
many wives and really loves one only).- cf. the Jacob story,
Gen.25-36. Ton.519 The home of the husband is the place
where one throws dry wood /the home of the bride is the
pot of water.(= A man gives everything nice he has to his
parents-in-law).

This proverb refers to the payment of bridewealth to the girl's family. "It
is no longer necessary to show that the African payment of bridewealth is
not a purchase. But to say that it is not price or purchase is not to say that
the objects handed over have no significance outside the particular purpose
they serve in bringing about a union. Cattle for Nuer are one of the main
sources of food and they supply many other domestic requirements, they
have a prestige value, and they have religious importance. The payment or
receipt of bridewealth changes a man's fortune in a very material way. The
bridegroom's family are impoverished, sometimes to the point of privation,
though their kinsmen and affines will help them if they reach this point;
while in the bride's home the milk-gourds and butter-gourds are full. A man
who receives only one cow of the bridewealth has in it the promise of a
herd."[30]

The payment of bridewealth also makes divorce very difficult. Among

(30) Evans-Pritchard, *Kinship*, p.89,

the Nuer not only the cattle but also the calves have to be returned. Evans-Pritchard reports a case of a divorce in which one of the bridewealth cows had to be returned with no less than eight calves - "and as these may have been widely dispersed much altercation may ensue....Everyone concerned with the marriage stands to lose by its dissolution and they will try to prevent divorce."[31]

Ton.525   The new field is not left idle /the fallow field is neglected.(= Greater regard is paid to the new wife of a polygamist). Ton.529 The ordeal is the woman.(= When adultery has taken place, a man is convicted by the woman's word). Fante p.524 A wife is like a blanket /for even though it scratches you /you are cold without it.- Similarly ibid. Even if a wife is unfaithful /you do not have to sleep alone.

Both Fante proverbs evaluate the pros and cons of marriage.

Bantu p.50   There is no end to an elephant.(= Do not marry in a hurry. There is plenty of time for such a big matter). ibid. A woman does not lie fallow.(= A woman will not lack men to marry her). Bav.25 He who casts out his hard-working wife does not laugh /he who has a contented wife laughs. Lov. p.152 We have no power / ask the girl.(= unwilling bride). Lov. p.158 About clothes you may say 'lend them to me' /but never about a woman.-This comparison reveals the African attitude that the woman is part of chattels and possessions. Kaf.(2) p.294 A stick has no kraal.(= Said of an irritable man who cannot obtain wives). Kaf.(2) p.296 The knife and the meat will never be friends.(= A warning against adultery). Aki. p.214 Two wives are two pots full of poison. Hausa 125 It is not the act of marrying that is difficult /it is getting the money (to marry).

While the proverbs of the previous section dealt with the institutions of marriage and divorce, the following are concerned with

c) the family (husband / wife)

According to Evans-Pritchard, a Nuer homestead, the home of a family, the household to which other kin may be attached, "consists of a byre and its attendant huts. The byre, a massive wattle-and-daub structure of some 15 to 20 feet in diameter, is the material and moral centre of the homestead. A

(31) Evans-Pritchard, *Kinship*, p.91,

man who builds a byre has started a family, herd, and home of his own. The byre stands for the father's status in the family. While he is alive his wives and sons and daughters are bound to him."[32]

Mal.1743 Equals are husband and wife /the little and the big are parent and child. Mal.1775 The wife is the mistress wished for /and the husband is master matchless.

The stability of the family increases a man's standing in the community:

Mal.1776 Loved by a spouse /so is able to talk. Mal.1781 What happens to your wife happens to yourself. Mal.1785 Family affairs should not be spread abroad. Mal.1786 Setting up house means the beginning of trial.

"A Nuer home is run by the combined efforts of all its members and the labour of running it is fairly distributed among them. One cannot but be struck by the camaraderie of the family as they assist one another in daily and seasonal tasks, either by direct aid or by co-ordination of activities. No work is considered degrading, no one is a drudge, all have leisure for rest and recreation, and all are content with their roles in the economy of the home."[33]

Mal.1787 Husbands and wives know each other's secrets. Mal.1791 Don't begrudge a spouse a good meal. Mal.1795 It is not smoke that warms the house /but agreement of husband and wife.

Mal.1797 At strife in the morning /at peace in the evening /at strife in the evening /at peace in the morning /like man and wife.- This proverb has the form of a riddle, with the last line containing the answer.

Mal.1798 Speak out when at home with your wife /or trouble will come on yourself. Mal.1800 A fierce fellow with one (wife) /for he hasn't two to be easily tamed.(= by making them jealous of one another).- Is this the Malagasy version of the 'Taming of the Shrew'? Mal.1801 A rival is not far off /for my brother's wife wears a red dress. Mal.1806 Even though agreed to by the husband /it isn't finished unless agreed to by the wife. Mal.1901 Have an elder brother and get a mentor /have a younger and get a porter. Mal.1902 A big elder brother is like a father. Ton.112 You have the trick of the *sanga* crab /which leaves its child and carries its male

(32) Evans-Pritchard, *Kinship*, p.124,
(33) Evans-Pritchard, *Kinship*, p.130,

on its back.(= Used by a husband when his wife does something which he does not like her to do). Ton.137 A cow will not fail to recognize her calf.(= A mother will not fail to recognize her child). Ton.177 One does not put the cat and the rat together.(= A man and a woman do not sleep in the same hut, if not husband and wife).

The following two proverbs state that the only one who cares for children is their own mother:

Ton.188   A chicken belonging to one hen /is not provided with grain by another hen.(= It is not the duty of a woman to look after another woman's child). Ton.189 The hen dead / the eggs rot.(= Children whose mother has died never find people who will really look after them).

Ton.252   The cricket sings in its hole.(= A man is king in his home). Ton.521 The soot in the roof of the hut is known by the owner.(= Quarrels between husband and wife are their own affair). Ton.522 The hut conceals many things.(= Family secrets are not disclosed outside). Ton.535 It is a woman who cooks for a husband she loves. Fante p.524 Do not tell your wife anything /that cannot be said in public. Lov. p.77 Love lies on the mother's side of the family / ownership on the father's.-

This proverb seems to reflect a patrilineal kinship system with marriage preferred to the matrilineal cross-cousin (mother's brother's daughter).

Lov. p.290   A woman's pubes may break up the family.(= Men are warned against the dangers of excessive promiscuity). Bech. p.199 Affairs of the family are not to be entered into (by strangers). Aki. p.214 A tree loses its blossom when bearing fruit.(= Beauty disappears when children are born). Aki. p.217 Starting a home is the beginning of troubles.ibid. Hurrah with mother and her faults!(= No one like mother). Aki. p.218 A home is not ruled by one who has not built it.(= master in his own house). Aki. p.219 A parent is merciful.(= A child can do no wrong). Aki. p.220 A parent does not discover the sugar canes' roots.(= Parents are always partial). Aki. p.223 The pup of the leopard claws like its mother.(= 'Like father like son'). Ewe 89 Your grandmother does not correct you /she sends you to your mother.(= 'Mind your own business'). Hausa 21 It is the

hen with chickens /that fears the hawk. Hausa 47 The
three cooking stones (i.e. the family) do not fail to give the
boy a coat.- cf. the Jabo proverbs on 'Solidarity and co-
operation'.[34]

Children have already been mentioned in the context of the family.
There are, however, some sayings which deal more specifically with

d) Children.

These are most numerous among the Tonga.

Ton.99   The little mouse does not forget its mother's way.(= A child
follows the ways of his father or mother). Ton.100 The
big mouse died bringing forth.(= When the child is bad he
brings trouble on his parents). Ton.186 The rooster does
not look after chickens.(= A man does not know how to
bring up children. It is the woman who brings up a child).
Ton.303 A hero begets a coward.(= Often a man's life and
habits are contradicted by his son's life and habits). Ton.450
= Bantu p.48 To bear children is wealth /to dress oneself
is (nothing but) colours. Ton.451 To bear children is
something clever.(= To have children is the greatest thing
in the world,... better than all wisdom). Ton.452 A good-
looking person will not give birth to handsome children.(=
Children do not often resemble their parents in their good
traits of character). Ton.453 One who has built a granary
/does not see his food eaten up by dogs.(= If a man has
children, his wealth will be properly looked after). Ton.455
To beget / the spirit vanishes.(= Said when you have
begotten a child and its deeds are at variance with its father's
spirit). Ton.456 Fire begets ashes.(= A father's deeds are
often contradicted by his son). Ton.458 The juice of the
mpfilwa tree comes from its stem.(= Children inherit the
faults of their parents). Ton.460 = Lov. p.110 The child
who cries is given food. Ton.461 Obedience is the crown
of a child. Ton.465 A single eye cannot see when it has a
grain of dust in it.(= It is a disability to have one child only).
Ton.469 In a mother's womb it is never two chiefs who
hurt.(= It is impossible that two nice and healthy children
be brought to light by one womb.... One example of the

(34) p.93

fear of twins). Ton.470 A childs hurts inside and outside
(the womb). Ton.472 A new barricade is strong /(when
strengthened) by an old one.(= A son is helped throughout
his life by his father).

According to Evans-Pritchard, Nuer boys come under their father's
direction - presumably after they have been weaned, i.e. at the age of three.
"He and the other men of the kraal see that they carry out their duties in the
care of flocks and herds. Boys learn from their elder brothers and cousins
how to fish, hunt, cultivate, dance, flirt, and engage in the other activities
of men. A boy can see the stages of his life before him - initiation, courtship,
marriage, and the starting of a family and home - and he realizes even in
childhood that these stages are bound up with his father's herd, and that he
and his brothers have a common interest with their father in the herd....

Boys treat their mothers with affection, though they are offhand with
them and are sometimes rude to them. When they are approaching the
threshold of manhood a feeling of male superiority seems to affect their
attitude to their mothers."[35]

Ton.474   A child forces you to eat out of a dirty pot.(= A child often
             brings shame to his parents). Ton.477 The infant makes
             laws.(= You are over-ruled by a small child. It imposes its
             will on the grown-up). Ton.482 Many children / many
             graves.(= high child mortality). Ton.518 To beget a
             woman is to beget a man.(= Do not grumble when you
             have begotten a woman, she will give birth to a man).
             Mal.1866 It is good to have wished for a child /and bear a
             boy. Mal.1869 Get many children /for some are sure to be
             good. Mal.1871 The cruel stepmother treats her children
             with partiality /though they are all hers.-In practice she
             cannot be bothered caring for the children of another wife.
             Mal.1875 The father is slandered /so the children are
             defamed. Mal.1876 Like a father and a mother /the one
             begat, the other nursed. Mal.1880 To have only one child
             /and be almost like the childless.- This is the reason why
             Rachel calls her first child 'Joseph' = may the LORD add
             another (Gen.30.24). Mal.1891 There is nothing so beloved
             as a child /but if it bites the breast /it is thrown off.-There
             is a limit to a child's behaviour. Mal.1893 If it cry after the
             mother /it wants the breast /if it cry after the father /it

---

(35) Evans-Pritchard, *Kinship*, p.138,

wants to go pick-a-back. Mal.1896 A playing with children:
Do it so as not to make them cry. Bav.15 The child of a
mouse never forgets its path.-Similarly with humans. Lov.
p.105 The stick even of a child /helps the adult across.
Bech. p.198 Children talk with God. Bech. p.200 Happy
is she who has borne a daughter /a boy is the son of his
mother-in-law.-

This saying seems to presuppose matrilocal residence.

ibid. The young bird doesn't crow /until it hears the old ones.Bech.
p.202 The antelope teaches its young to leap.Bech. p.203 A lion never
breeds a leopard.-

Or the same positively:

Kaf.(2) p.296 He is a calf of an old cow. Chag.9 The ox rewards with
kicks.(= An undutiful child who responds to parental care
with stubbornness and disrespect). Chag.19 He who
leaves a child / lives eternally.(= Man lives on through his
descendants). Kam.4 The mother of the ram has no
horns.(= Said of a woman of plain looks ... who has a
handsome or gifted son). Kam.5 The guineafowl bears a
francolin.(= A favourite saying, when a good man has an
unworthy son).- cf. Ezek.18.10-13. Aki. p.222 The son
for whom his father works the field /does not know that
things are precious.-Cf. the sluggard in Prov.10ff. Nandi
2 The lion bears a hyena.(= A son is unworthy of his
father). Nandi 7 They send hares to the elephant /(not
elephants to the hare).(= It is the duty of children to wait
on elders, not elders on children).

As the Hebrew Bible is particularly concerned with widows and orphans
as poorly protected members of society (cf. Isa.1.17 et al.), there is also in
Africa a group of proverbs referring to the

e) Orphan.

The widow by contrast seems to be better protected, be it through
levirate marriage or through return to her kin.

Mal.1903   An orphan with a big spoon /he profits by his poverty
(eating all he can). Mal.1904 Like the ravenous orphan: /
his means are gone /and there is none to advise moderation.
Mal.1908 When those who have fathers are offered advice
/it is the orphans who get it first.(= need it most). Kundu

473 Rainy season - orphan.(= The dark rainy season with little food is likened to a life in poverty, as the orphan leads it). Kundu 506 Ediki: not the former.(= It is said of the people of Ediki ... that in former times they were very stupid and were often taken for a ride. The saying is applied to an orphan who as an adult does no longer like to be bossed around, while in his youth he was pushed around and taken advantage of). Kundu 536 An orphan never opposes the village. Kundu 1232 An orphan longs for his mother's food. Kundu 1233 An orphan does not put a large rod into running streams.-This proverb is used concerning orphans and poor people in general. (= A poor man cannot stand up to respected people).

Another person to be pitied is

f) the barren woman.

The biblical figures of Sarah, Rachel, and Hannah make us aware of the suffering of barren women in Israel. Five Malagasy proverbs reflect a similar attitude:

Mal.1858   The barren woman is disliked by her husband /and dies before she is called 'Beloved'. Mal.1859 The barren woman is in a sad case /for she catches locusts for the children of another. Mal.1860 The barren woman is a withered tree /when she dies she goes altogether. Mal.1861 The barren woman is in a sad case /for she saves for the children of her rival. Mal.1862 To have no family /like a barren sheep.

Similarly the following Tonga proverbs:

Ton.136   A cattle kraal is not strong without a calves' kraal.(= A village without children is a dreadful thing). Ton.204 = Bantu p.48 A guinea-fowl without chickens /is nothing but colours only.(= If a woman is very beautiful but has no children, she is of no use).- Cf. Bantu p.48 To bear children is wealth / to dress oneself is nothing but colours.

Looking back on the material that deals with family and kinship in the Old Testament and in the proverbs of Africa, we find both agreement and disagreement. To begin with, the African material is not homogeneous, because it is derived from societies which are based on patrilineal, matrilineal, or double descent. But, the Bible also displays a variety of kinship structures.

While in the Jacob-Laban story (Gen.29-31) the children of two wives and two handmaids are clearly Jacob's children (patrilineal descent), he nevertheless pratises uxorilocal, or better: avuncolocal, residence in the home of his mother's brother. And while for Jacob it is the patrilineage that counts, this view is not shared by Laban: "The daughters are my daughters and the children are my children" (Gen.31.43). It is, therefore, methodologically correct to look at the full breadth of African proverb material when comparing it to the Bible, and not to eliminate societies based on matrilineal or double descent in favour of those whose kinship system is patrilineal and whose residence is patrilocal.

As we might have expected, a large group of sayings in Prov.10-29 deals with education, but not - and here the evidence contradicts most Old Testament scholars - with school education! Education is the task of the family. Mother is in charge of small children and the daughters, and father takes charge of the boys probably at the age of three. A sensible son should listen to his father's instruction, and the consequences of ignoring it (poverty, disgrace) are painted in glaring colours. Whip and rod can be used, if all else fails, but neglecting the education of the child brings shame to the parents. This section overlaps twice with 'Wisdom and folly', which is indicated by the fact that both the pairs 'wise/foolish' and 'father/mother' are used in Prov.15.20; 17.25.

To set up home and to start a family one first needs to find a good wife. But judging by the warnings given (Prov.21.9,19; 25.24; 27.15+16), many an Israelite seems to have ended up with a contentious one. All the more they sing the praises of the good one (Prov.12.4; 18.22; 19.14; 31.10-31), who comes ultimately from the LORD. The *Yiddishe Momme* is her modern secular descendant.

The proper functioning of the family is based on respect of the children for their parents (Prov.19.26; 20.20; 28.24), and of the young for the old (17.6; 20.29), and on kinship solidarity (17.17; 18.19). The latter is extended even to the slave when he becomes part of the family. One generally sticks close to home and does not travel much (27.8). All these sayings and the ideals they represent have hundreds of parallels in Africa.[36]

(36) This is confirmed both by specialist investigations of proverbial material, such as Milimo on the Plateau Tonga and Herzog on the Jabo, and by the field work done by Evans-Pritchard among the Nuer of Sudan and by Esther Goody among the Gonja of Northern Ghana: "In seeking to understand the factors involved in the establishment of a marriage, it is important to recognize that the families of *bride* and *groom* (my italics) have very different points of view, though they share the hope that the marriage, when

finally settled on, will be amicable and fertile. For the *bride's* people it is the right to give or withhold consent to their daughter's marriage that is the chief concern. They may wish to see her married to a kinsman, or to a friend and ally. Or they may simply wish to be sure that her husband is a man of good character, and one who will respect his parents-in-law. ... The *husband's* kin, on the other hand, have the problem of incorporating a stranger into their domestic life. Many of the variations noted in elements of marriage ritual relate to the special ways of integrating the bride in her new surroundings. ... The emphasis on courtship with its provision for winning the consent of the girl and her parents, and the recognition of a common minimal element (the marriage kola) as the formal criterion of marriage are both consistent with, and indeed facilitate, open connubium. They are both concerned with the proper *establishment of relationships* between individuals, spouses and affines, rather than with the transfer of rights over women between descent groups." (E.N. Goody, *Contexts*, p.101).

7

Creation and Wisdom

I intend to approach this topic by asking four questions: (1) 'What exactly is Wisdom?' A question to which we all thought we had the answer. (2) 'What is the specific method of Wisdom?' Here a glance at modern Physics might be helpful. (3) 'What is the function of creation in Wisdom thought?' The theological answer to this question is still given from within an Old Testament context, while (4) 'What is the role of Wisdom in Theology?' now clearly moves the issue into the field of systematics.

(1) What exactly is Wisdom?

Let us start off with a preliminary working definition: I shall refer to all such parts of the Old Testament as 'Wisdom' in which knowledge is not acquired through a process of revelation, but through the rational application of the human mind. Within the context of the Hebrew Bible the Books of Proverbs, Job, and Ecclesiastes would first of all have to be mentioned, although it would be somewhat artificial to exclude Sirach (Ecclesiasticus) and Wisdom of Solomon from our consideration. And there are 'Wisdom' sections in other parts of the Old Testament too, notably in the Psalms.[1] Starting with simple proverbs, it is not easy to say who coined them and how they became part of the Hebrew Bible. Let us look at a few examples from Prov.10:

'A wise son makes a glad father / but a foolish son is a sorrow to his mother' (v.1) 'Treasures gained by wickedness do not profit' (v.2) 'He who winks the eye causes trouble' (v.10) 'A slack hand causes poverty' (v.4) 'A son who gathers in the summer is prudent / but a son who sleeps in the harvest brings shame' (v.5) 'A stitch in time saves nine' or 'An apple a day

---

(1) R.N.Whybray, *The Intellectual Tradition in the Old Testament*, BZAW 135, 1974.

keeps the doctor away'!

Maybe two of those were not from Prov.10 – but, as you notice, they could have been!

So we can observe straight away that there is no great difference between Hebrew and English proverbs (or German and African ones for that matter). Even today Prov.15.1 is still used in correspondence: 'A soft answer turns away wrath'. So at first sight it would appear that in all these cases we are dealing with folk proverbs.

But this is not what standard Old Testament scholarship tells you.[2] It would appear that a complete mythology has grown up in Old Testament research in relation to Wisdom. It is assumed that there was a hypothetical class of 'wise men' attached to the court who taught in equally hypothetical 'schools', and that their teaching consisted of the class ethics of the civil service ('*Beamtenethik*'). Let us for the moment stick to common sense and not confuse fact and fiction.

While we know of the wise woman from Tekoa (II Sam. 14), who was used by Joab in order to persuade David to bring the banished Absalom back to Jerusalem, the evidence for a class of 'wise men' is rather thin on the ground. R.N.Whybray has clearly shown that the Hebrew word *hakham* has the same meaning as 'wise' or 'intelligent' in English.[3] It is a human quality and not a job. Counsellors, diplomats, and civil servants were wise and intelligent. But their profession was that of counsellors, diplomats, and civil servants and not that of wise men or intellectuals.

Whybray has even provided a satisfactory explanation for Jer. 18.18, which mentions priests, prophets, and wise men together. But priests, prophets, and wise men are not mentioned in Jer. 18 because they are three professions: what they have in common is rather that they are the ones who are forever talking.[4]

What then about the connection of Wisdom with the royal court? Here it is important to distinguish between the *origin* and the *collection* of proverbs. I am not denying that proverbs were *collected* at the royal court – where else? (cf. Prov. 25.1) – but what we are discussing is the question of their *origin*. I have carried out a detailed study of the royal and court sayings in Israel and Africa.[5] The result of this was that for the African proverbs popular origin is either highly probable or virtually certain. Prov. 10-29 shows a similar

(2) Cf. G. von Rad: *Weisheit in Israel*, 1970 (ET: *Wisdom in Israel*, 1972).

(3) Whybray, *Int. Tradition*, pp.6-54.

(4) Whybray, *Int. Tradition*, pp.24-31.

(5) Cf. The Royal and Court Sayings ..., pp.16-35.

picture: There is not *one* single royal or court saying in the case of which popular origin is excluded. When the sayings are critical of the court or king, popular origin is very probable. The African parallels suggest to me that it is much more likely for the royal and court sayings to have originated among ordinary people rather than at court, because their perspective is that of the commoner and not that of the courtier. We may therefore conclude that the origin of Wisdom at the royal court, claimed or just repeated by so many scholars, cannot be proved from the royal and court sayings. The great majority of these sayings rather supports the common sense argument for the *popular* origin of proverbs.

What then about schools in ancient Israel? That there is no biblical evidence for the existence of schools in Israel during the monarchy and that the first mention of a school occurs in the 2nd century BC (Eccl.us 51.23) – 800 years after Solomon! – has been pointed out by me elsewhere.[6] The 'school myth' was first propagated by A.Klostermann (FS Zahn 1908). He claimed that there were three biblical texts which presupposed the existence of schools in Israel: Prov. 22.17-21; Isa. 28.9-13 and 50.4-9. The first passage is an excerpt from the Egyptian papyrus *Amen-em-ope*, which reflects the existence of schools in Egypt, but proves nothing for Israel. The second passage refers to parents (baby talk) and small children of pre-school age, while the third is an exilic (!) Servant Song dealing with prophetic discipleship and not with schools. Hence Klostermann's often repeated 'evidence' for schools is worthless.

Archaeology, too, has provided no evidence for schools either. The few pitiful scraps that have been found can easily be explained by the master-apprentice system (often: master = father) under which young Israelite scribes were trained. This position has been vigorously contested by A.Lemaire,[7] as I had quite unintentionally pulled the plug on his book, in which he attributes pretty well the origin of the whole Bible to the hypothetical schools.[8] David's and Solomon's cabinet lists (II Sam. 8.15-18; 20.23-26; I Kings 4.2-6) provide no joy either, as a 'head of school' is never mentioned.

It is therefore easier to assume popular origin for the Hebrew proverbs, rather than to take refuge in unproven hypotheses. The 'men of Hezekiah' (Prov. 25.1) and their work is probably comparable to that done by the

---

(6) Cf. The Israelite Wisdom School ..., pp.4-15.
(7) Cf. his anti-Golka, "Sagesse et écoles", *VT* 34, 1984, pp.270-81.
(8) A.Lemaire, *Les écoles et la formation de la Bible dans l'ancient Israel*, Fribourg / Göttingen 1981.

brothers Grimm with their collection of German fairy tales – of which they are also not the authors. Late 8th century BC Judah also went through a phase of nationalism and a similar romantic movement. This is probably the reason why Hezekiah carried out a collection of proverbs, in pursuit of the popular spirit ('*Volksgeist*').

How then did these anonymous folk proverbs find their way into the canon of the Hebrew Bible? They were, no doubt, much helped by pseudonymous attribution to Solomon. It has to be borne in mind that the Hebrew canon did not develop all in one go. When the Samaritans dropped out of mainstream Judaism, only the Pentateuch was regarded as authoritative, while Jesus refers to the Hebrew Bible of his time as 'the Law and the Prophets'.[9] The third section of the canon, the Writings of which the Wisdom books form a part, was not defined until Judaism was challenged by early Christianity. But it is of ecclesiological significance for both that in Proverbs not only the experiences of an intellectual élite were included, but that the book voices the experiences of God and life of very ordinary people. But it needed the protection of Solomonic pseudonymity for the lower strata of society to be able to make their contribution.

(2) What is the specific method of Wisdom?

Stephen W. Hawking in his book, *A Brief History of Time*, describes physical theories as follows: "Any physical theory is always provisional, in the sense that it is only a hypothesis: you can never prove it. No matter how many times the results of experiments agree with some theory, you can never be sure that the next time the result will not contradict the theory."[10] This could be a description of the observations and maxims of Wisdom.

"On the other hand", says Hawking (ibid), "you can disprove a theory by finding even a single observation that disagrees with the predictions of the theory." This happens in the case of Job, where one of the classic three righteous men (Ezek. 14.14) has been chosen in order to dislodge the hypothesis of an act-consequence relationship. The defensive strategy against this method of falsification (Karl Popper) is the same in Physics as in Hebrew Wisdom: "You can always question the competence of the person who carried out the observation" (ibid). And this is exactly the strategy employed by Job's friends, who demand that he should confess the sins which he has so far failed to acknowledge.

(9) Mt. 5.17; 7.12; 11.13 et al.
(10) S.W.Hawking, *A Brief History of Time. From Big Bang to Black Holes*, London 1988, p.10.

This empirical approach of Hebrew Wisdom agrees with that of Science against the Aristotelian tradition which held "that one could work out all the laws that govern the universe by pure thought: it was not necessary to check by observation."[11] Hebrew Wisdom proceeds more like an empirical science, purely on the basis of observation. If Plato's account of Socrates in the early dialogues is correct, there would be stronger similarities between this Greek philosopher and Hebrew Wisdom. Socrates, like the Hebrew sages, follows the inductive principle. He builds up a theory (e.g. that of *arete*) from countless empirical observations, rather than deducing individual applications from a general theory.

Hebrew Wisdom is rather cautious with generalizations. There seems to be continuous astonishment that there is a correspondence between the animal world and that of humans (the ant / the industrious person). Similarly a relationship is established between the world of plants and that of humans. The proverbs explore the world of nature and that of human nature - they represent an elementary stage of the natural and social sciences.

Physics is keen to uncover a set of laws, within the limits set by the uncertainty principle, according to which the universe will develop. Hebrew Wisdom does the same, with YHWH's will providing the ultimate uncertainty principle. From a Wisdom point of view theology and science are in the same boat. The whole medieval problem of faith and reason never even comes in sight. Science is doxology, it traces the footprints of the creator in creation.

Maybe the only clear example where Wisdom has ever gone beyond the limits of restricted observations is the theory of the so-called act-consequence relationship, which says that it was found to be true that the righteous flourish and the wicked come to a bad end. This does not imply reward and punishment, rather that the good person creates such a sphere of goodness around him/her that his/her fellow human beings can simply not fail to respond equally to all this goodness, the opposite being true for the wicked. While many a psalmist is troubled by the non-working of this theory (or providing interim comfort: *respice finem!*), it would be wrong for us to assume that this observation is simply a mistake. It was found to be true by generation after generation.

But just at this point we see clearly that Wisdom, like Physics, is capable of self-correction. The case of the righteous man Job provides indeed the one example necessary to falsify the theory. Job is clearly righteous, and yet he suffers. And the author of the book makes the argument even more

(11) Hawking, *Time*, p.15.

watertight. Having stated that Job himself was a godfearing man (1.1-3), he then proceeds in vv. 4+5 to show that Job did not suffer on account of his children either, because he performed sacrifices for them after each of the dinner parties they used to give in turn in their houses. Hence the act-consequence relationship must eventually fall in the Book of Job - only to be resurrected in Sirach and Wisdom of Solomon in different political circumstances on the strength of fresh evidence.

One other key doctrine might be worth a mention: the doctrine of the right time, treated comprehensively in the poem Eccl. 3.1-8, with the rest of the chapter as commentary. Here again scholars would claim that this doctrine shows a court background. The courtier needs to know the right time when to speak before the king. True, but what a bourgeois view of things! In most societies, Israel, Africa or ancient Sumer (the Sumerian proverbs date from the 3rd millennium BC!) it is the farmer in the first instance who needs to know the right time for seed and harvest. Proverbs probably spread like agriculture from Mesopotamia through the Fertile Crescent into Northern Africa and Europe. Hunter societies (Eskimos, Red Indians) have virtually no proverbs. So it is from the farmer's world that the concern for carrying out the right action at the right time penetrates everybody's daily life. And this task was not beyond human wit. It just needed the application of the brain or else the rod (Prov. 29.15).

While Ecclesiastes upholds the orthodox doctrine of the right time, he clearly has serious epistemological problems with it. He admits that God 'has made everything to suit its time' and also that 'he has given men a sense of time past and future'; but then he drops the epistemological clangour: 'but no comprehension of God's work from beginning to end' (Eccl. 3.11). Ecclesiastes is playing Space Invaders blindfold and not enjoying it.

Let it finally be said that Hebrew Wisdom is not, like Physics, after a Grand Universal Theory (= GUT). Its ultimate uncertainty principle is YHWH. 'The plans of the mind belong to man / but the answer of the tongue is from the LORD', Prov. 16.1. 'Many plans are in the mind of a man / but it is the pupose of the LORD that will be established', Prov. 19.21. The Akikuyu have a similar saying: 'The designs of one's heart do not arrive / but those of God arrive'.[12] So, while Wisdom is optimistic about the pursuit of knowledge, it is nevertheless clearly aware of its limitations.

(12) C.Cagnolo, *The Akikuyu. Their Customs, Traditions and Folklore*, 1933, p.218.

(3) What is the function of creation in Wisdom thought?

Already one quick glance at the Book of Proverbs teaches us that the term 'creation' is an inadmissible generalization – exegetes and systematicians are equally guilty here. In Proverbs the creation of the world and that of man are *never* mentioned together. I am here much indebted to the work of a fellow Westermann pupil, Peter Doll,[13] who observed that the two occur in different parts of Proverbs. The creation of man (with apologies to the feminists, but 'creation of humanity' really will not do, as it is always the individual who is addressed and not humanity as such) occurs in individual proverbs within the collection Prov. 10-29, while the creation of the world can be found in the larger poems of Prov. 1-9.[14]

The creation of man figures very prominently in the sayings concerned with rich and poor:

Prov. 14.31 He who oppresses a poor man insults his maker / but he who is kind to the needy honours him. Prov. 17.5 He who mocks the poor insults his maker / he who is glad at calamity will not go unpunished. Prov. 22.2 The rich and the poor meet together / the LORD is the maker of them all.

These proverbs are being used to defuse conflict, to minimalize social tension. As the small farmer is a fellow creature, there are limits to his exploitation. God as his creator guarantees the human dignity of the poor person. Doll suggests that these sayings might have been uttered by socially responsible elders who intend to emphasize the equality of rich and poor before their maker. "The rich can claim no greater right before God, the creator, than the poor. This saying intends to encourage the poor to show the rich their limits. The equality of creation urges the abolition of the class structure and gives the community a chance to solve its conflicts of interest on this basis."[15]

Other proverbs concerning rich and poor (10.4; 16.26; 28.19, etc.) show a similar picture, as do the ones about the industrious and the idle (sluggard). Similarities with Amos' social criticism suggest that these proverbs might well have been used during the early monarchy, although the presence of similar proverbs among the tribes of Africa shows that they derive from the earlier tribal society in Israel (contra Doll). This society was a guardian of

---

(13) P.Doll, *Menschenschöpfung und Weltschöpfung in der alttestamentlichen Weisheit*, Stuttgart 1985.
(14) Creation of man = Prov. 14.31; 16.4; 17.5; 20.12; 22.2; 29.13 and creation of the world = Prov. 3.19f; 8.22-31.
(15) Doll, *Menschenschöpfung*, p.19.

equality, while the monarchy tended to increase the class divisions.

It seems to me then that Doll has shown that the creation of man, whose original *Sitz im Leben* is the Individual Lament,[16] has its main function as a part of social criticism. Even the poorest person is protected from exploitation and oppression by the fact that he or she is God's creature. This was at least the theory: Israel's practice, alas, was often quite different.

Let us now turn to the creation of the world. There is no reference to it in Prov. 10–29 in the self-contained individual proverbs. But reference to the creation of the world is made in the Wisdom poems of Prov. 1–9, viz. in 3.13–26 and chapter 8. Outside the Book of Proverbs Job 28 is the most outstanding Wisdom poem that makes reference to the creation of the world. The origin of the creation of the world is the motif of God's majesty in the Descriptive Psalm of Praise (Hymn). God's might and majesty (as opposed to his mercy and kindness) are manifest in the act of the creation of the world. Prov. 1–9 show a noticeable shift in their understanding of Wisdom in comparison with chapters 10–29. Wisdom now becomes the concern of human thinking, which is quite inconceivable for the simple proverbs. It is a principle of order which leads to blessing. One could almost say that the human interest moves away from YHWH to Wisdom. But as opposed to the Egyptian goddess *Ma'at*, who represents the principle of cosmic and social order, Wisdom's role remains clearly related to and derived from YHWH:

> Prov. 3.19f The LORD by wisdom founded the earth / by understanding he established the heavens; by his knowledge the deep broke forth / and the clouds drop down the dew.

But in this process Wisdom has become more and more a partner in creation (*co-creatrix*). This is even more clearly expressed in

> Prov.8.22: The LORD created me at the beginning of his work, the first of his acts of old,
>
> 23: Ages ago I was set up, at the first, before the beginning of the earth.
>
> 24: When there were no depth I was brought forth, when there were no springs abounding with water,
>
> .. ..
>
> 30: then I was beside him, like a master workman; and I was daily his delight, rejoicing before him always,
>
> 31: rejoicing in his inhabited world and delighting the sons of men.

The creation of the world is obviously regarded as a complete process.

---

(16) C.Westermann, *Lob und Klage in den Psalmen*, Göttingen 1977, and R.Albertz, *Weltschöpfung und Menschenschöpfung*, Stuttgart 1974.

But, nevertheless, YHWH still remains its Lord and Master, as is made clear in the parallel poem Job 28:

25: When he gave to the wind its weight, and meted out the waters by measure;

26: when he made a decree for the rain, and a way for the lightning of the thunder;

27: then he saw it and declared it; he established it, and searched it out.

28: And he said to man, 'Behold, the fear of the LORD, that is wisdom; and to depart from evil is understanding.'

We have therefore, according to Doll,[17] in these poems a tradition of the creation of the world which originally derives from Descriptive Praise (Hymn), but which in these poems has achieved a certain degree of independence in the praise of Wisdom.

While it is no longer possible to separate the creation of man and the creation of the world quite so neatly in the deutero-canonical Wisdom books, we are at least able to say for Proverbs that the creation of man functions as part of social criticism, while the creation of the world belongs to the Descriptive Praise of God. While Wisdom in the latter remains clearly subordinate to God, it takes on a certain degree of independence.

The creation of the world is then the *conditio sine qua non* of all Wisdom thinking, in Israel as well as elsewhere in the Ancient Near East. The fact that the world is created guarantees order (*Ma'at, cosmos*), and where there is order knowledge and understanding are possible. This is ultimately Job's final comfort.

It has often been noticed that in the divine speeches in the book (chapters 38–41) Job does not really receive an answer to his questions. YHWH seems almost to crush him with his divine omnipotence manifest in the wonders of creation and to take no notice of Job's undoubtedly valid objections. Job has to concede in the end: 'I know that thou canst do all things, and that no purpose of thine can be thwarted' (42.2). And he apologizes for having spoken out of turn. But what looks to us like a capitulation, is really something quite different for Job. Granted, Job's questions do not receive an answer, but God addresses him personally in an almost pastoral way. And from this address Job is able do derive the comfort that the principle of order still stands. So he, the troubled individual, is actually able to shelve his own problems and leave his fate in the hands of his creator – who, of course, does

(17) Doll, *Menschenschöpfung*, p.58.

him proud in the end. Divine omnipotence as a source of trust and comfort?[18]

The importance of the creation of the world in Wisdom thought becomes even more obvious in the Book of Ecclesiastes. Theologically it is almost Ecclesiastes' last stand. Having failed to perceive the rule of God in human lives (Ecclesiastes' epistemological problem), he nevertheless places great trust in the creator. First of all, he feels awe in God's presence: 'I know what ever God does lasts forever; to add to it or to subtract from it is impossible. And he has done it all in such a way that men must feel awe in his presence' (Eccl. 3.14). Secondly, this trust in the creator is a source of joy for Ecclesiastes: 'I know that there is nothing good for man except to be happy and live the best life he can while he is alive' (Eccl. 3.12). This is the reason why it is ultimately futile to draw comparisons between Ecclesiastes and modern Existentialism (Sartre, Camus). Camus' appeal to Sisyphos to keep on rolling back the stone – and hence make an ethical decision in the face of absurdity – is not Ecclesiastes' position. He remains a theist, even where he fails to comprehend God's activity in life. The road to atheism is simply not open to him – nor probably to any ancient man for that matter – because it is blocked by his understanding of the world as having been created. Hence there is order (*cosmos*, as the Hellenists would have said) at least on the divine level, even if epistemological difficulties prevent Ecclesiastes from perceiving this order in his own life. All is vanity? Maybe not quite all.

(4) What is the role of Wisdom in Theology?

This, of course, is the most difficult question. How am I going to perform this quantum leap from historical description to constructive theology? I think I had better do it in small instalments.

a) Looking at various aspects of a sapiential creation Theology, the first which springs to mind is *ecology*. When the world we live in is understood as created, this invariably limits our rights as inhabitants of this earth. We are not owners, but stewards. *Dominium terrae* can therefore only mean stewardship and never exploitation. The species (human, animal and plant) which proverbial Wisdom observes are a product of God's blessing.[19] Wisdom looks at human beings in their natural communities (family,

---

(18) Cf. G. van den Brink, *Almighty God. A Study of the Doctrine of Divine Omnipotence*, Kampen, 1993.
(19) Cf. the biblical Primeval history, Gen. 1-11.

neighbourhood, clan, village), at old and young, generation after generation. Hence the need to make provision for oneself, for one's descendants, and ultimately for the whole planet earth. In facing the ecological issue Theology will have to pay heed to Wisdom texts dealing with the creation of the world. This also lifts the relevant texts in Gen. 1-11 out of their 'primeval' isolation. The Wisdom approach is proof that the Primeval history does not talk about 'once upon a time', but about our world here and now, as it is - and, of course, as it ought to be.

b) We notice in Wisdom literature as well as in the Primeval history that these texts deal with human beings as such, not with the Israelites, but with the whole of humanity. An important aspect of Wisdom theology is its *universalism*. One could mention the Book of Jonah in this context.[20] In Jonah, too, the creator refuses to destroy his creatures (this is the significance of the '120,000 persons ... and also much cattle' in 4.11). A theology which takes the creation of humanity and of each individual seriously will balance its statements about the old and new Israel with those about the whole of humankind.[21]

c) Once we accept that the root of the tradition of the creation of man is in *social criticism*, these texts will have to play a much larger part in the social and ethical concerns of Theology (this should make a nice change from the inevitable Amos!). After the celebrations of the bicentenary of the French Revolution it seems proper to remind ourselves that such ideas as human rights, fraternity, and equality are more than 3000 years old. It is even more obvious from the American Declaration of Human Rights that they can ultimately only be justified on the basis that all human beings are God's creatures. There is no completely secular foundation of human rights, at least to my knowledge.

A theology based on the creation of man in Prov. 10-29 would also have to be more critical of some of the developments in our Western societies. To say it quite bluntly: The spirit of unrestrained enterprise capitalism is compatible neither with Judaism nor Christianity. As God's creatures rich and poor are brothers, they both have the same maker. This fact prohibits the exploitation of the poor and warns the rich against despising the lower strata of society. It also restricts the exploitation of animals, because they too, are God's creatures.

(20) Cf. my commentary 'Divine Repentance' in G.A.F.Knight - F.W.Golka, *Revelation of God, The Song of Songs & Jonah*, ITC, Grand Rapids/Edinburgh, 1988.
(21) For details cf. F.W.Golka, "Universalism and the Election of the Jews", *Theology*, July 1987, pp.273-80.

d) Hebrew Wisdom is the popular predecessor of Philosophy; it is also dedicated to the pursuit of *knowledge*. So, apart from the revealed faith, there is apparently a direct appeal to the human mind to penetrate the created order of the cosmos. This appeal and the love of knowledge are almost erotic features in Wisdom literature. Hebrew Wisdom clearly envisages a natural theology, but cannot conceive of this ever coming into conflict with revealed faith. Israelite faith is never afraid of reason. The two must ultimately lead to the same goal, God the creator. The fact that Hebrew Wisdom has made little contribution to recent theology is probably due to the Barthian *anathema* against natural theology. I detect, however, signs that the need to respond to the ecological crisis and the need to co-operate with all persons of good will (theists and non-theists) is forcing Theology in a different direction.

e) This observation also has a spin-off with regard to the problem of *other faiths*. In the field of Wisdom it is sometimes impossible to draw a distinction between biblical and non-biblical material. African proverbs are similar to Hebrew ones and biblical instructions are often modelled on Egyptian or Mesopotamian ones. Nearly all nations on earth refer in their traditions to our earth as created by the/a deity. This indicates to me that there is a great similarity among the peoples of this earth with regard to their 'primeval' traditions and also their standards of social behaviour expressed in proverbs. This is a fact which has been insufficiently reflected by contemporary theology. But again the global ecological problems (rain forest) force upon Theology a global strategy which may need a broader basis than the Judaeo-Christian revelatory tradition.

f) Finally, if my claim, made in the face of traditional scholarship, is true, viz. that in Prov. 10-29 quite *ordinary people* (as opposed to courtiers!) have made a contribution to the Hebrew Bible of Judaism and to the Old Testament of the Christian church, be it only under the cover of Solomonic pseudonymity, and that these ordinary people have found their way into the canon of two world religions, then the Synagogue and the Church need to take this phenomenon seriously. Are both institutions today speaking in a language which reaches ordinary people? It could be that the plain person has given more to Judaism and Christianity than they have to him or her.

Appendix

The Biblical Joseph Story and Thomas Mann's Novel

When an Old Testament scholar tackles such a subject, he can claim expertise as far as Gen 37-50 is concerned, but he remains a layman when it comes to the Germanistic aspect of his topic. A German scholar would be in no better position, were he to attempt an interpretation of the biblical Joseph story. Manfred Dierks, the Thomas Mann expert and my Oldenburg colleague, has kindly given me some help, but nevertheless, this remains the paper of an Old Testament scholar whose love for biblical narrative art has led him to Thomas Mann.

I shall begin by sketching the main lines of interpreting the biblical Joseph story, although Thomas Mann remained quite untouched by standard German Old Testament scholarship. It would have been of little help to him. For his biblical background Mann consulted the work of an outsider in our discipline, Alfred Jeremias, whose book, *Das Alte Testament im Lichte des alten Orients*, Leipzig 1904, he used. Alfred Jeremias belongs to the school of the so-called Panbabylonists who explained the Old Testament exclusively against the background of Babylon. More about him later. Mann was further influenced by the anthropologist Edgar Dacqué (*Urwelt,Sage und Menschheit*, 1924). Mann's understanding of myth was influenced by the works of Dmitri Mereschkowski which appeared between 1903 and 1924. But, as Manfred Dierks has shown, it is impossible to understand Thomas Mann without Schopenhauer's philosophy, Nietsche's critique and the *Leitmotiv*, as used by Richard Wagner.

But back to the Old Testament. The late 19th century's understanding of the biblical Joseph story is best demonstrated by J.Wellhausen's work, *Die Composition des Hexateuchs*, 1866 and 1877 respectively. For Wellhausen the Hexateuch, of which the Joseph story forms a part, is a work of literature consisting of four continuous written sources. This implies that our Joseph

123

story originated as a combination of literary sources into a new unified whole. This cannot be completely wrong, because, as opposed to other parts of the Hexateuch, the Joseph story shows clear signs of literary composition.

What then is Wellhausen's view and dating of these sources which he needs for his reconstruction of the Israelite-Jewish history of religion? The oldest source he calls "Yahwist" (abbreviated: J from the German *Jahwist*) after the Hebrew divine name *Yahweh*. He dates it in the 9th century B.C., the time after the division of the united monarchy. This Yahwist is supposed to be located in the Southern kingdom, i.e. in Judah, presumably at court in Jerusalem. To this Yahwist Wellhausen attributes a continuous theological-literary composition, ranging from the creation story in Gen. 2 to the narratives of the conquest of the land in the Book of Joshua. The spirit of this work is universalistic, liberal, and orientated towards Jerusalem. In the Joseph story it is the emphasis on the role of Judah among the brothers - as opposed to Reuben, the eldest - which Wellhausen regards as the work of his Judaean Yahwist.

According to Wellhausen, this Yahwistic work has been revised during the 8th century in the Northern kingdom. This revision he calls "Elohist", after the Hebrew word *elohim* = God, because this conservative editor avoids the divine name. The conservative character of E is illustrated by the fact that this work has no Primeval history. It talks about the election of Abraham and his descendants without having mentioned, like J, God's blessing for all his creatures. This would be explicable against the background of the rejection of everything Canaanite by the 8th century prophets in North Israel. In the Joseph story Wellhausen attributes the lion's share of the material to E. The spokesman of the brothers is Reuben, the eldest. E, too, is apparently meant to be a work from the election of Abraham to the conquest. This, however, has always been questioned by scholarship.

Wellhausen's third source is D, Deuteronomy. He identifies it with Josiah's law-book which was found in Jerusalem during the 7th century, although it may well originally derive from the North. As D is confined to the Book of Deuteronomy, it is of no significance for the Joseph story.

Wellhausen's fourth and last source is the Priestly code (P). It reflects the theological interests of the second temple congregation, e.g. the sacrificial cult. In the Joseph story P hardly plays any part, except as part of the final form of the Hexateuch, which Wellhausen attributes to a redactor R^JEDP.

This gives us Wellhausen's complete four-sources theory (abbreviated: JEDP), normally referred to as "documentary hypothesis". But does the Joseph story give the impression that it has been put together by a redactor from various literary sources, or is it rather a unity, a well planned composition, the work of a literary genius? Thomas Mann instinctively sided with the latter position.

Wellhausen himself realizes how a serious this problem is. I quote him from the *Composition des Hexateuchs* on Genesis 37-50: "The main source even for this latter part of Genesis is JE. Presumably this work has here as everywhere been put together from J and E; our previous results demand this assumption and would be badly shaken, were they to be proved wrong (in the Joseph story)"[1]. But can Wellhausen's assumptions be confirmed by the Joseph story? I myself do not think so. Wellhausen describes the Yahwist's contribution, J, as a continuous work, which the Elohist worked over later on, i.e. E presupposes J. But in the Joseph story the relationship of both groups of texts to each other is exactly the reverse! Its continuous thread of narration is that of the Elohist (who avoids the divine name and makes Reuben the spokesman of the brothers) - Wellhausen's supposedly younger source! This narrative has later been revised by a Yahwist (who uses the divine name and makes Judah the spokesman of the brothers) - Wellhausen's supposedly older source! This reverse relationship between J and E disproves in my opinion Wellhausen's documentary hypothesis for the Joseph story. I should abandon it for the rest of the Pentateuch as well, as the connections between the Yahwistic and Elohistic passages in the various cycles and saga clusters of the Pentateuch which Wellhausen claimed have never been proved by him.

That this means the end of the documentary hypothesis, but not of the literary critical method, has been clearly shown by my Oldenburg predecessor, Walter Dietrich, in: *Die Josephserzählung als Novelle und Geschichtsschreibung*.[2] Once the exegete has abandoned the blinkers of the documentary hypothesis, he suddenly appreciates the genius of the Joseph narrator. In Germany the dominance of Wellhausen was first of all broken by Hermann Gunkel's form-critical method. In several editions of his Genesis commentary around the turn of the century Gunkel voices his thesis: "Genesis is a collection of sagas", i.e. in the first place oral tradition! This put an end to the tyranny of Wellhausen's sources. While Gunkel allows them to continue, they became quite unimportant for him, as the narratives had received their decisive form and development at the stage of oral tradition. Gunkel paints a lively picture of the origin of the saga clusters of Abraham,

---

(1) J.Wellhausen, *Die Composition des Hexateuchs und der historischen Bücher des Alten Testaments*, 3rd edn 1899 (reprint: Berlin 1963), p. 52.

(2) *Zugleich ein Beitrag zur Pentateuchfrage*, Neukirchen-Vluyn 1989.

Isaac and Jacob.[3]

But what did Gunkel's form-criticism contribute to our understanding of the biblical Joseph story? Very little! With his form-critical method Gunkel always pursued the quest for the smallest possible units: the story, the song, the proverb or the prophetic oracle. The Joseph story, however, does *not* consist of such small units, rather it is a novelette, a carefully planned structure. It did not originate through oral tradition, but has already been conceived as a literary work. If Thomas Mann was looking for the genius of the Joseph narrator, he could not expect much help from this Old Testament scholar either.

In Old Testament research, tradition-history took the place of form-criticism. It came too late for Thomas Mann, because, after a short trip to Palestine in 1925, he began writing his Joseph novel in 1926. *The Stories of Jacob* appeared in 1933. Previously, in 1930, Mann had undertaken some further extended travelling through Palestine and Egypt. But in many ways and at many places Thomas Mann anticipated the results of tradition-history.

In Germany this method is inseparably bound up with the name of Martin Noth. Due to the war Noth's 'Tradition-history of the Pentateuch' could only appear in 1948.[4] In it Noth builds on the oral tradition and its saga clusters established by Gunkel. This leads him to a new view of the Patriarchal history.

Genesis presents the Patriarchs as a family of three generations, whereby Abraham has become Isaac's father and Jacob's grandfather. This is a technique of the Genesis narrator. He combines independent saga clusters by turning their heroes into relatives. Thus Moses, Aaron and Miriam have become brothers and sisters, Abraham and Lot uncle and nephew, and Jacob and Esau also brothers. Once this technique of the narrator has been understood, it becomes apparent that the Jacob stories, favoured by Thomas Mann, form the oldest part of the Patriarchal history. Jacob was the Patriarch of Central Palestine and Transjordan. Abraham and Isaac belong to the South. Here, however, the tradition of the younger Abraham group seems to have pushed out that of the older Isaac people almost completely. Stories with Isaac as their hero are confined to Gen. 26. Otherwise he is only born, nearly sacrificed, and finally married off.

Hence we note without surprise that the Patriarchal history narrates the

(3) H.Gunkel, *Die Genesis*, Göttingen 6th edn 1964 = 3rd edn 1910 (ET: *The Legends of Genesis*, Chicago 1901).

(4) M.Noth, *Überberlieferungsgeschichte des Pentateuch*, Stuttgart 1948; ET: *A History of Pentateuchal Traditions*, Englewood Cliffs 1972.

same things again and again, because all three Patriarchs are founders of a cult. Their descendants venerate the god of their father. All three migrate in the quest for land, and the continuation of their families is always in danger, be it through famine - a central motif in the Joseph story - or their own stupidity. But the promise of the respective Patriarchal God is with all three Patriarchal groups, and their continuation is a sign of his blessing. God's blessing here means fertility of humans and animals.

This principle of repetition in the Patriarchal narratives can also be found in Thomas Mann's novel, as Manfred Dierks showed in his contribution to the 1986 Thomas Mann colloquium in Lübeck.[5] Joseph quasi relives the experiences of Abraham, Isaac and Jacob. A servant Eliezer re-appears anew in each generation. He has a somewhat floating identity. He smiles at us from each epoch of early history: "Here I am again!" He is a type like the Patriarchs themselves.

Where did Mann get this principle of repetition from, if he was not influenced by Noth's tradition-history? According to Dierks, Thomas Mann's work also narrates the philosophy of Schopenhauer. In this case the Joseph novel deals "with human self-liberation from the confinement to mythological predestination ... and in the end with a fairy-tale like floating of the individual between predestination and self-determination".[6] Mann uses the term "myth" in such a way "that basically all beings in the world are only one".[7] The biblical Patriarchal history here meets the philosophy of Schopenhauer and his interpretation of the *world as will and imagination*. According to Dierks, both for Schopenhauer and Thomas Mann "not the individual, but the thing as such 'behind it' is real".[8] This brings back memories of Plato's doctrine of ideas and of the medieval argument about the universals. Of course, Schopenhauer's conclusion that the thing as such is ultimately nothing would have been drawn neither by Plato nor by the author of Genesis.

Hence Schopenhauer's philosophy is reflected in Thomas Mann's narrative style, which the biblical material facilitates. According to Dierks, this philosophy "puts a kind of semantic net over the world, which holds it together".[9] In order to achieve this coherence Thomas Mann systematically

(5) M.Dierks, "Über einige Beziehungen zwischen psychischer Konstitution und 'Sprachwerk' bei Thomas Mann", in: Internationales Thomas-Mann-Kolloquium 1986 in Lübeck, *Thomas-Mann-Studien* VII, Bern 1987, p.273.

(6) ibid.

(7) ibid.

(8) Dierks, *Thomas-Mann-Studien* VII, p.274.

(9) Dierks, *Thomas-Mann-Studien* VII, p.282.

creates repetition. To quote Manfred Dierks again: "This of course is Schopenhauer's method of presentation: Each individual phenomenon of the world of imagination is reduced to the fundamental truth of the will, which is always the same. Thus he describes the coherence of the world".[10]

We therefore discover a strange parallel movement between the Patriarchal history, as sketched by Martin Noth, and the principle of repetition, as applied to these Patriarchs by Thomas Mann, although there was never any connection between the two. While the result of our investigation of the influence of main line Old Testament research on Thomas Mann has so far been purely negative, we must now turn to the one and only scholar, Alfred Jeremias, whose work, *Das Alte Testament im Lichte des alten Orients*, Mann used.

As already noted, Jeremias belongs to the so-called Panbabylonists, who explained the Old Testament predominantly against its Babylonian background. Mann learned from Jeremias that Babylonian religion was an astral religion. This is important e.g. in Joseph's dream, when sun, moon and eleven stars bow to him. Also Mann's description of the biblical Primeval history was strongly influenced by Jeremias. Mann's description of Joseph's beauty not only displays homoerotic features - Joseph is more than Tadzio - but it is based on the figure of Tammuz, about whom Mann learned from Alfred Jeremias. Tammuz is the young dying and rising vegetation god. Joseph's colourful garment and the fact that he is thrown into the pit point in this direction. Thomas Mann and Alfred Jeremias are united by their common interest in myth, which is again and again made new by the principle of repetition.

The Panbabylonists, of whom Jeremias was one, achieved some notoriety when one of their number, Friedrich Delitzsch, on 13th January 1902 posed the question in a public lecture in Berlin: Can the Bible still be regarded as divine revelation when it becomes apparent that the Babylonian stories of creation and flood are older than the biblical ones? His own answer was clearly negative and later on enthusiastically taken up by the Nazis. Alfred Jeremias differs from Delitzsch insofar as he emphasizes the superiority of the biblical accounts over the Babylonian ones. He also remains on good terms with the Church by means of his christological interpretation.

It was during Thomas Mann's conservative, 'non-political' period that he was influenced by Alfred Jeremias. Thomas Mann later abandoned this position and, during the rise of the Nazis, actively defended the Weimar republic. Jeremias's influence decreased in the later volumes of *Joseph*. The

(10) ibid.

third volume, *Joseph the Provider*, written in American exile and published in 1943, shows quite different features, viz. those of Franklin Delano Roosevelt and his 'New Deal'.

While the influence of Old Testament scholarship on Thomas Mann was mainly negative, with the exception of Alfred Jeremias, we may well ask whether Mann's novel in turn stimulated Old Testament research. In Gerhard von Rad's case this was clearly so. Von Rad was not only guided by Thomas Mann in his search for the literary genius of the biblical Joseph author, but he also discussed this relationship in his essay, "Biblische Josephserzählung und Josephsroman", of 1965.[11]

Von Rad's epochmaking study of the Joseph story appeared in 1953. In his article, "Josephsgeschichte und ältere Chokma",[12] von Rad explains the origin of Gen. 37-50 from the spirit of ancient wisdom, and he regards Joseph as the exemplary wise man. This article is only 7 1/2 pages long, and von Rad does not quote Thomas Mann's novel. I am therefore unable to prove that von Rad actually knew the novel in 1953. Gerhard von Rad, however, was a person of immense literary education, who in his younger years in Jena had connections with the circle around Ricarda Huch. As the Joseph novel appeared between 1933 and 1943, I think it almost impossible that in 1953 it should have been completely unknown to von Rad.

This is in my opinion supported by the fact that in the Chokma article Thomas Mann's quest for the spirit of the biblical Joseph material meets with von Rad's own interest in Hebrew wisdom. Von Rad, however, gives a much more secular interpretation of the Joseph story than Thomas Mann whose special interest is myth. According to von Rad, Joseph represents the ideal of wisdom education: discipline, modesty, friendliness and self-control. As ancient wisdom and the Joseph story make few theological statements, as both relegate God's activity to a radical hiddenness, distance and unknowability, von Rad comes to the conclusion: "The Joseph story with its clear didactic tendencies belongs to the teaching of older wisdom."[13] This means paradoxically that von Rad as a theologian has a much more secular understanding of the Joseph material than Thomas Mann.

This becomes even more apparent in his essay of 1965, "Biblische Josephserzählung und Josephsroman", in which von Rad expressly deals with Thomas Mann. To begin with, von Rad offers in two parts an analysis of the biblical narrative and of Thomas Mann's novel respectively. Von Rad

(11) In: G. von Rad, *Gottes Wirken in Israel*, ed. O.H.Steck, Neukirchen-Vluyn 1974, pp. 285-304.

(12) In: G. von Rad, *Gesammelte Studien zum Alten Testament*, München 1965, pp.272-80.

(13) *Ges. Studien*, p.279.

regards as the didactic purpose of the novel the relevance of mythic realities. Thomas Mann himself referred to his *Joseph* as a "manifestly mythological work".[14]

It is about the application of this word "myth" that von Rad argues with Mann. As basic to myth he regards its ritual magic performance. "The existence of the world and its order is always in danger. Hence it becomes necessary to secure this world order – or even to re-create it – by reciting or performing this sacred myth. In Thomas Mann's novel the events follow the same law of repetition."[15] The characters of the novel therefore never experience anything really new. With B.Richter[16] von Rad finds the fate and feelings of the characters of the novel "fixed in roles", they only respond to "events which are familiar since time immemorial".[17]

While Thomas Mann regards myth as "open to the past"[18] the biblical story, according to von Rad, is radically open to the future: "To the same degree in which the characters of the novel are searching *for* or finding their justification *in* the myth – whereby they meet the divine sphere in mythical primeval orders – the gulf increases between the novel and the Old Testament ..., because there humans are justified and protected by a salvation event which is itself irreversible and creates irreversible facts."[19]

This sounds like the old cliché of the Old Testament's linear understanding of time as opposed to the cyclical way of thinking in the Ancient Near East, the perpetual return of everything, an idea to which Thomas Mann was still attached. Here we must disagree with von Rad. Of course, the Old Testament has a linear understanding of time, and history is indeed open to the future. But, at the same time, there is a cyclical experience of time, in the cycles of the week and of the year, in the cult and in the festivals. Von Rad has in my opinion fallen for the linear understanding of history of Barthian theology. Thomas Mann saw things quite correctly, while in poetic licence he gave them a somewhat one-sided emphasis. The investigation of the relevance of myth in the work of the older Thomas Mann, demanded by von Rad, has since then been provided my Manfred Dierks in his thesis, *Studien zu Mythos und Psychologie bei Thomas Mann*[20] – although Dierks of

(14) vol. XI, p.630.
(15) *Gottes Wirken*, p. 296.
(16) "Der Mythosbegriff Thomas Manns und das Menschenbild der Josephsromane", *Euphorion* 1960, pp.411ff, esp. p.420.
(17) von Rad, *Gottes Wirken*, p.297.
(18) *Adel des Geistes*, p.582.
(19) von Rad, *Gottes Wirken*, p.302.
(20) Freiburg 1972.

course would not claim theological competence.

Despite these disagreements it is quite apparent how much von Rad was influenced by Thomas Mann in his quest for the spiritual world of the biblical Joseph story and the literary genius of its author. But was he always able to maintain this approach consistently? Has he not relapsed in his Genesis commentary, where Yahwist and Elohist seem miraculously to re-appear, into the Wellhausian documentary hypothesis?

This is exactly the criticism of von Rad made by Norman Whybray.[21] If on the one hand we are to believe that the Joseph story is a literary masterpiece, then it is on the other hand hardly credible that such a masterpiece should have been put together from two different novelettes. Von Rad's results do indeed call into question the documentary hypothesis. But he still seems to have been too frightened to take the logical step of abandoning it altogether.

But this is exactly what Herbert Donner[22] attempted to do in his paper to the Heidelberg Akademie der Wissenschaften of 11th January 1975: "From all that we know about the character and the narrative technique of the old Pentateuchal sources we are forced, on the basis of G. von Rad's formcritical definition and new interpretation, to draw the conclusion which he himself was not prepared to draw. You cannot have it both ways: either the Joseph story is a novelette or it is part of the Pentateuchal sources J and E. It is either still a saga cluster like the Abraham - or more so the Jacob - stories; then we could indeed expect it in a Yahwistic or Elohistic version. Or it is a novelette in the sense of G. von Rad, in which case it belongs neither to J nor E, but is a literary entity in its own right."[23]

Donner endorses the criticism of Whybray whom he quotes. But more important is perhaps the fact that from now on German Old Testament scholars have been influenced not only by von Rad's classic analysis, but also by Thomas Mann's novel. Donner begins his paper with the last words of the novel: "Die schöne Geschichte und Gotteserfindung von Joseph und seinen Brüdern".[24]

On the basis of the Joseph story Donner then refutes all the criteria which have so far been adduced for the necessity of a source division. This is particularly well illustrated by his treatment of the doublets. The latter are

(21) R.N.Whybray, "The Joseph Story and Pentateuchal Criticism", *VT* 18, 1968, pp.522-28.

(22) *Die literarische Gestalt der alttestamentlichen Josephsgeschichte*, Heidelberg 1976.

(23) Donner, *Josephsgeschichte*, p.14.

(24) "The beautiful story and divine invention of Joseph and his brothers", Donner, *Josephsgeschichte*, p.7.

part of the narrative technique of the novelette - a point on which Donner was inspired by Thomas Mann - and must not be explained away by the assumption of two sources: "The Joseph novelette has a noticeable predilection for the number two. To mention just a few things: Joseph's dreams before his brothers, the dreams of the court officials in prison, and Pharaoh's dreams all appear in pairs; Joseph is imprisoned twice, in the cistern and in his Egyptian prison; his brothers travel twice to Egypt; there are two attempts to take Benjamin, the youngest, with them to Egypt; twice the money paid for the grain is secretly put back into the brothers' sacks; during both of their visits to Egypt the brothers are twice received by Joseph; and it would appear that Jacob and his sons are twice invited to settle in Egypt."[25] According to Donner, the doublets serve for emphasis or in order to delay the action.

This one example must suffice. If, after Donner's refutation of the source division in the Joseph story, one now expects radical theses on Pentateuchal criticism, the mountain only gives birth to a mouse: While the redactor has replaced the Yahwistic and Elohistic Joseph narratives by our novelette, it is now claimed that he did use the two sources in Gen. 1-36 and later on again in Exodus! Wellhausen needs to be saved from himself. While the old master had claimed that the Pentateuchal sources could either be found in the Joseph story or not at all, we are now told by Donner: The Pentateuchal sources do not exist in the Joseph story, but before and after it you can carry on as usual! A poor result, considering that Donner takes Thomas Mann's novel as his starting point.

Perhaps my Oldenburg predecessor, Walter Dietrich, was more successfully inspired by Thomas Mann. His recent study of Gen. 37-50 bears the title *Die Josephserzählung als Novelle und Geschichtsschreibung* (1989). Its subtitle, *Zugleich ein Beitrag zur Pentateuchfrage*, leads one to expect not an all-out attack on Wellhausen's documentary hypothesis, but certainly some criticism of it. Dietrich, too, refers to Wellhausen's all-or-nothing quotation on JE in the Joseph story. When he says (on p.18): "Does one not scar and destroy such a finely woven artifice as the Joseph story by applying to it the tools of historical criticism, and in particular literary criticism?" this comes close to heresy for a former Göttingen scholar! And this can hardly be regarded as a one-off aberration by the Göttingen inquisition, because Dietrich incriminates himself even further: "The most beautiful and profound interpretations of the Joseph story have been written by authors

(25) Donner, *Josephsgeschichte*, p.36f.
(26) Dietrich, *Josephserzählung*, p.12.

who have taken little or no notice of source criticism."[26] Dietrich mentions the Jewish commentary *Genesis Rabba*, Calvin's interpretation of Genesis, and Thomas Mann's "great novelistic trilogy". Further literature is mentioned in the footnotes, and such a suspect work as Robert Alter's *The Art of Biblical Narrative* (1981) can hardly have escaped the attention of the inquisition.

Dietrich's ultimate denial of his Göttingen roots follows on the same page (12): "Those who assume the existence of the old Pentateuchal sources - not those who do without them - have the onus of proof on their side" - sentences more familiar from Rolf Rendtorff or the present writer.[27]

How strongly Dietrich was influenced by Thomas Mann, can be seen from his use of the *Leitmotiv*, where he is also indebted to George W. Coats.[28] Coats, of course, is an old Heidelberger. Dietrich no longer attributes repeatedly occurring colourful clothes, dreams etc. to different sources, but he recognizes their *Leitmotiv* character. He abandons his scholarly ancestors, Wellhausen - Martin Noth - Rudolf Smend in favour of Richard Wagner, Thomas Mann and George Coats. Dietrich defines the Joseph novelette in relation to Thomas Mann's novel. The art of omitting everything "which Thomas Mann tells us almost excessively"[29] is characteristic of Gen. 37-50. Characteristic of the literary genre of the novelette is a technique of reduction. While a novel paints a picture of the time and the circumstances of life, the novelette limits itself to a section of the same.

How does Dietrich solve the problem of the apparently competing doublets 'Midianites/Ishmaelites', 'Reuben/Judah' and 'Jacob/Israel'? While Donner denied their character as doublets, Dietrich tries to explain it historically. He assumes that an original Joseph novelette has been re-worked later on as historiography.

This Joseph novelette Dietrich attributes to the time of the early North Israelite monarchy. The first North Israelite king, Jeroboam I, had to flee to Egypt, but nevertheless became king later on. The image of the monarchy, as represented by Joseph, was, according to Dietrich, shaped by humane and social ideals: "This is obviously an ideal self-portrait which the early Northern monarchy painted of itself."[30] After the collapse of the Northern kingdom many Israelites fled to Judah, bringing, according to Dietrich, the

---

(27) Rolf Rendtorff, *Das überlieferungsgeschichtliche Problem des Pentateuch*, BZAW 147, 1977; F.W.Golka: Art. "German Old Testament Scholarship", in: *Dictionary of Biblical Interpretation*, eds. R.J.Coggins & J.L.Houlden, London / Philadelphia 1990, pp. 258-64.

(28) G.W.Coats, "Redactional Unity in Genesis 37-50", *JBL* 93, 1974, pp. 15-21.

(29) Dietrich, *Josephserzählung*, p.17.

(30) Dietrich, *Josephserzählung*, p.66.

Joseph novelette with them. There it was turned into historiography under the influence of the Story of David. In Judah both Joseph and David were portrayed according to the ideal of the beautiful young man. This younger version shows more scepticism and distance towards Egypt. According to Dietrich, the guilt standing between the brothers has become more serious. Judah overtook all the brothers and became their spokesman and leader. It is Dietrich's thesis that the Joseph historiography has been deliberately modelled on the David historiography.

Dietrich does not tell us what he imagines the relationship of the Joseph novelette and historiography respectively to the remainder of the Pentateuchal tradition to be like. His quoting of the Wellhausian all-or-nothing demand with regard to Gen. 37-50, however, seems to indicate, that he, too, thinks that the axe has already been put to the root of the documentary hypothesis.

I have so far ignored two major contributions, as they hardly refer to Thomas Mann and relate to Egyptology in which I have no expertise. The important monograph by Donald Redford, *A Study of the Biblical Story of Joseph*,[31] points to Egyptian habits and customs in Gen. 37-50 which can hardly have existed before the time of the Persians or Ptolemies. This would put W.Dietrich's dating into question again. But only a competent Egyptologist could settle this dispute.

Arndt Meinhold - first of all in his Greifswald thesis of 1971 and then in two *ZAW* articles[32] - follows Redford's late dating. He regards the Joseph story as well as the Book of Esther as diaspora novelettes. There are two critical questions I should like to ask Meinhold:

(1) Why does he ignore the parallel between Gen. 37-50 and the Book of Daniel where a Jewish exile also rises at a foreign court through his interpretation of dreams?

(2) The Joseph story has *one* hero, but the Book of Esther has *two*, Esther and Mordecai. Does this not put the supposed parallel into question?

In summary: Our review of the Joseph exegesis has shown that since G. von Rad German Old Testament scholarship has been spellbound by Thomas Mann's novel. Under his influence scholarship moved more and more away from Wellhausen's sources and has gradually adopted a holistic interpretation of Gen. 37-50. It was Thomas Mann who broke the tyranny of the documentary hypothesis. I am therefore bold enough to claim that Thomas Mann made an important contribution to German Old Testament scholarship.

(31) (Genesis 37-50), *SupplVT* 20, Leiden 1970.
(32) "Die Gattung der Josephsgeschichte und des Estherbuches: Diasporanovelle I & II", *ZAW* 87, 1975, pp. 306-24 and *ZAW* 88, 1976, pp. 72-93.

Bibliography

Albertz, R. *Weltschöpfung und Menschenschöpfung*, Stuttgart 1974.

Avi-Yonah, M. (ed). *Encyclopedia of Archaeological Excavations in the Holy Land* 2, London 1976; vol.3 ed. by Avi-Yonah and E.Stern, 1977.

Brink, G. van den. *Almighty God. A Study of the Doctrine of Divine Omnipotence,* Kampen 1993

Brown, Tom. *Among the Bantu Nomads*, London 1926 (= Bech.).

Brunner, H. *Altägyptische Erziehung*, Wiesbaden 1957.

Bullock, C. *The Mashona. The Indigenous Natives of S. Rhodesia*, Cape Town and Johannesburg 1927 (= Mash.).

Cagnolo, C. *The Akikuyu. Their Customs, Traditions and Folklore*, Nyeri/ Kenia 1933 (= Aki.).

Christensen, J.B. "The Role of Proverbs in Fante Culture", in: E.P. Skinner (ed), *Peoples and Cultures of Africa*, New York 1973, pp.509ff (= Fante).

Coats, G.W. "Redactional Unity in Genesis 37-50", *JBL* 93, 1974, pp.15-21.

Comaroff, John L. (ed). *The Meaning of the Marriage Payments*, London et al. 1980.

Crenshaw, J.L. "The Influence of the Wise upon Amos", *ZAW* 79, 1967, pp.42-52.

Crsemann, F. *Der Widerstand gegen das Königtum. Die antiköniglichen Texte des Alten Testaments...*, Neukirchen-Vluyn 1978.

Dierks, M. "Über einige Beziehungen zwischen psychischer Konstitution und 'Sprachwerk' bei Thomas Mann", in: Internationales Thomas-Mann-Kolloquium 1986 in Lübeck, *Thomas-Mann-Studien* VII, Bern 1987.

Dierks, M. *Studien zu Mythos und Psychologie bei Thomas Mann*, Freiburg 1972.

Dietrich, W. *Die Josephserzählung als Novelle und Geschichtsschreibung.*

Zugleich ein Beitrag zur Pentateuchfrage, Neukirchen-Vluyn 1989.

Doll, P. *Menschenschöpfung und Weltschöpfung in der alttestamentlichen Weisheit*, Stuttgart 1985.

Donner, H. *Die literarische Gestalt der alttestamentlichen Josephsgeschichte*, Heidelberg 1976.

Driver, G.R. *Semitic Writing from Pictograph to Alphabet*, 2nd edn, London 1954; now in 3rd edn (1976).

Duhm B. *Das Buch Jesaja*, Göttingen, 5th edn 1968 = 4th edn 1922.

Dundas, C. *Kilimanjaro and its People*, London 1924 (= Chag.).

Dürr, L. *Das Erziehungswesen im Alten Testament und im antiken Orient*, Leipzig 1932.

Ellis, A.B. *The EWE-Speaking Peoples*, London 1890 (= Ewe).

Erman, A. "Das Weisheitsbuch des Amen-em-ope", *OLZ* 27, 1924, col.241-52.

Erman, E.A. "Eine ägyptische Quelle der Sprüche Salomos", *SAB* 1926, pp.86-93, Tab. VI-VII.

Evans-Pritchard, Sir Edward. *Kinship and Marriage among the Nuer*, Oxford 1966 = 1951.

Evans-Pritchard, Sir Edward. *The Nuer. A Description of the Modes of Livelihood and Political Institutions of a Nilotic People*, Oxford 1968 = 1940.

Evans-Pritchard, Sir Edward. *Witchcraft, Oracles, and Magic among the Azande*, Oxford 1976.

Finnegan, Ruth. *Oral Literature in Africa*, Oxford 1970.

Fohrer, G. *Das Buch Jesaja* 2, Zürich 1962, vol. 3, 1964.

Fontaine, Carole R. *Traditional Sayings in the Old Testament*, Sheffield 1982.

Fox, Robin. *Kinship and Marriage. An anthropological Perspective*, Penguin, Harmondsworth, Middlesex 1967.

Gerstenberger, E. *Wesen und Herkunft des "apodiktischen Rechts"*, WMANT 20, Neukirchen-Vluyn 1965.

Gerstenberger, E.S."Der Realitätsbezug alttestamentlicher Exegese", *SVT* 36, 1984, pp.132-44.

Golka, F.W. "Die Königs- und Hofsprüche und der Ursprung der israelitischen Weisheit", *VT* 36, 1986, pp.13-36.

Golka, F.W "Die israelitische Weisheitsschule oder 'Des Kaisers neue Kleider'", *VT* 33, 1983, pp.257-70.

Golka, F.W. "Universalism and the Election of the Jews", *Theology*, July 1987, pp.273-80.

Golka, F.W. "Die Flecken des Leoparden. Biblische und afrikanische Weisheit im Sprichwort", *Schöpfung und Befreiung*, ed.s R. Albertz, F.W.

Golka, J. Kegler, Stuttgart 1989, pp.149-65.

Golka, F.W. Art. "German Old Testament Scholarship", in: *Dictionary of Biblical Interpretation*, ed.s R.J. Coggins & J.L. Houlden, London/ Philadelphia 1990, pp.258-64.

Golka, F.W. *Die biblische Josefsgeschichte und Thomas Manns Roman*, Oldenburger Universitätsreden Nr.45, Oldenburg 1991.

Goody, E.N. *Contexts of Kinship. An Essay in the Family Sociology of the Gonja in Northern Ghana*, Cambridge 1973.

Gottwald, N.K. *The Tribes of Yahweh. A Sociology of the Religion of Liberated Israel 1250-1050 B.C.E.*, London 1979.

Gressmann, H. "Die neugefundene Lehre des Amen-em-ope und die vorexilische Spruchdichtung Israels", *ZAW* 42, 1924, pp.272-96.

Gressmann, H. *Israels Spruchweisheit im Zusammenhang der Weltliteratur*, Berlin 1925.

Gunkel, H. *Die Genesis*, Göttingen 6th edn 1964 = 3rd edn 1910 (ET: *The Legends of Genesis*, Chicago 1901).

Hambly, W.D. *The Ovimbundu of Angola*, Chicago 1934 (= Ovim.).

Hawking, S.W. *A Brief History of Time. From Big Bang to Black Holes*, London 1988.

Hermisson, H.-J. *Studien zur israelitischen Spruchweisheit*, Neukirchen-Vluyn 1968.

Herzog, G. *Jabo Proverbs from Liberia. Maxims in the Life of a Native Tribe*, Oxford/London 1936 (= Jabo).

Heusch, Luc de. *Why Marry Her? Society and Symbolic Structures*, Cambridge 1981.

Hildebrandt, Ted. "Compositional Units in Proverbs 10-29", *JBL* 107, 1988, pp.207-24.

Hollis, A.C. *The Masai. Their Language and Folklore*, Oxford 1905 (= Masai).

Hollis, A.C. *The Nandi. Their Language and Folklore*, Oxford 1969 = 1909 (= Nandi).

Horst, F. "Die Doxologien im Amos-Buch", *ZAW* 47, 1929, pp.45-54.

Houlder, J.A. *OHABOLANA or Malagasy Proverbs I and II*, Antananarivo 1915/16; French translations by H. Noyer (= Mal.).

Ittmann, J. *Sprichwörter der Kundu (Kamerun)*, Berlin 1971 (= Kundu).

Jeremias, A. *Das Alte Testament im Lichte des Alten Orients*, Leipzig 1904.

Junod, H.P. and Jaques, A.A. *The Wisdom of the Tonga-Shangaan People*, Cleveland/Transvaal 1936 (= Ton.).

Junod, H.P. *Bantu Heritage*, Johannesburg 1938 (= Bantu).

Kidd, Dudley. *The Essential Kafir*, London 1904 (= Kaf.2).

Klostermann, A. "Schulwesen im alten Israel", *FS Theodor Zahn*, Leipzig 1908. pp.193–232.

Knight, G.A.F. and Golka, F.W. *Revelation of God, The Song of Songs & Jonah*, ITC, Grand Rapids/Edinburgh, 1988.

Krige, E.J. and J.D. *The Realm of a Rain-Queen*, London 1943 (= Lov.).

Lévi-Strauss, *The Elementary Structures of Kinship*, London 1969.

Lemaire, A. *Les écoles et la formation de la Bible dans l'ancient Israel*, Freiburg/ Schweiz and Göttingen 1981.

Lemaire, A. "Sagesse et écoles", *VT* 34, 1984, pp.270–81.

Lindblom, G. *Kamba Folklore III*, Uppsala 1934 (= Kam.).

McCall, G. *Kaffir Folk-lore*, 1892 (= Kaf.).

McKane, W. *Proverbs*, London 1970.

Meinhold, A. "Die Gattung der Josephsgeschichte und des Estherbuches: Diasporanovelle I & II", *ZAW* 87, 1975, pp.306–24 and *ZAW* 88, 1976, pp.72–93.

Melland, F.H. *In Witch-bound Africa*, London 1923 (= Lunda / Kaonde).

Merker, M. *Die Masai*, 1904 (= Mas.).

Messenger jr., John C. "The Role of Proverbs in a Nigerian Judicial System", *Southwestern Journal of Anthropology* 15, 1959, pp.64–73 (= Anang).

Middleton, J. and Tait, D. (ed.s). *Tribes Without Rulers. Studies in the African Segmentary Systems*, London 1958.

Milimo, J.T. *A Study of the Proverbial Lore of the Plateau Tonga of Zambia*, B.Litt. thesis, Oxford 1976 (= Tonga).

North, C.R. *The Second Isaiah*, Garden City, New York 1968.

Noth, M. *Überlieferungsgeschichte des Pentateuch*, Stuttgart 1948; ET: *A History of Pentateuchal Traditions*, Englewood Cliffs 1972.

Otto, E. *Ägypten - Der Weg des Pharaonenreiches*, Stuttgart, 2nd edn 1955.

Pedersen, Joh.s. *Israel. Its Life and Culture I-II*, London/Copenhagen, 1926.

Perdue, L.G. *Wisdom and Cult*, Missoula / Mont. 1977.

Plöger, O. *Sprüche Salomos (Proverbia)*, BK XVII, Neukirchen-Vluyn 1984.

Procksch, O. *Jesaja I*, Leipzig 1930.

Rad, G. von. *Theologie des Alten Testaments*, vol.1, Munich, 6th edn 1969 = 4th edn 1962 (ET: *Old Testament Theology*, vol. I, Edinburgh and London 1962).

Rad, G. von. "Josephsgeschichte und ältere Chokma", in: *Gesammelte Studien zum Alten Testament*, Munich 1965, pp.272–80.

Rad, G. von. *Weisheit in Israel*, Neukirchen-Vluyn 1970 (ET: *Wisdom in Israel*, Nashville, Tennessee 1972).

Rad, G. von. "Biblische Josephserzählung und Josephsroman", *Gottes Wirken in Israel*, ed. O.H. Steck, Neukirchen-Vluyn 1974, pp.285-304.

Radcliffe-Brown, A.R. and Forde, D. *African Systems of Kinship and Marriage*, Oxford 1950.

Rattray, R.S. *Hausa Folk-lore II*, Oxford 1913 (= Hausa).

Raum, O.F. *Chaga Childhood*, London 1940.

Redford, D.B. *A Study of the Biblical Story of Joseph (Genesis 37-50)*, SVT 20, Leiden 1970.

Redford, D.B. "Studies in relations between Palestine and Egypt during the First Millennium B.C.", in: J.W. Wevers and D.B. Redford (ed.s), *Studies in the Ancient Palestinian World*, Toronto 1971, pp.141-56.

Rendtorff, R. *Das überlieferungsgeschichtliche Problem des Pentateuch*, BZAW 147, Berlin and New York 1977.

Richter, B. "Der Mythosbegriff Thomas Manns und das Menschenbild der Josephsromane", *Euphorion* 1960, pp.411ff.

Ringgren, H. *Sprüche*, Göttingen, 3rd edn 1980.

Roscoe, John. *The Baganda*, London 1911 (= Bag.).

Roth, W.M.W. "The Numerical Sequence x/x+1 in the Old Testament", *VT* 12, 1962, pp.300-11.

Schapera, I. "Tswana Legal Maxims", *Africa* 36, 1966, pp.121-34 (= Tswana).

Skladny, U. *Die ältesten Spruchsammlungen in Israel*, Göttingen 1962.

Spieth, J. *Die Ewe-Stämme*, 1906, pp.599-612.

Stayt, H.A. *The Bavenda*, London 1931 (= Bav.).

Vaux, R. de. *Ancient Israel. Its Life and Institutions*, London, 2nd edn 1965.

Wallis, E.A. *Facsimiles of Hieratic Papyri in the British Museum*, Second Series, London 1923, Tab. I-XIV and pp.9-11; 41-51.

Wellhausen, J. *Die Composition des Hexateuchs und der historischen Bücher des Alten Testaments*, 3rd edn 1899 (reprint: Berlin 1963).

Westermann, C. *Jesaja 40-66*, Göttingen 1966.

Westermann, C. "Weisheit im Sprichwort", *Forschung am Alten Testament* 2, Munich 1974, pp.149-61.

Westermann, C. *Lob und Klage in den Psalmen*, Göttingen 1977.

Westermann, C. *The Parables of Jesus in the Light of the Old Testament*, Edinburgh 1990.

Westermann, C. *Wurzeln der Weisheit. Die ältesten Sprüche Israels und anderer Völker*, Göttingen 1990.

Whybray, R.N. "The Joseph Story and Pentateuchal Criticism", *VT* 18, 1968, pp.522-28.

Whybray, R.N. *The Intellectual Tradition in the Old Testament*, BZAW 135, Berlin 1974.

Whybray, R.N. *Wealth and Poverty in the Book of Proverbs*, JSOT Suppl 99, Sheffield 1990.

Wolff, H.W. *Amos' geistige Heimat*, WMANT 18, Neukirchen-Vluyn 1964.

Abbreviations of African Proverb Collections

Aki. see Cagnolo, C.

Anang see Messenger jr., John C.

Bag. see Roscoe, John.

Bantu see Junold, H.P.

Bav. see Stayt, H.A.

Bech. see Brown, Tom.

Chag. see Dundas, C.

Ewe see Ellis, A.B.

Fante see Christensen, J.B.

Hausa see Rattray, R.S.

Jabo see Herzog, G.

Kaf. see McCall, G.

Kaf.2 see Kidd, Dudley.

Kam. see Lindblom, G.

Kaonde see Melland, F.H.

Kundu see Ittmann, J.

Lov. see Krige, E.J. and J.D.

Lunda see Melland, F.H.

Mal. see Houlder, J.A.

Mas. see Merker, M.

Masai see Hollis, A.C. *The Masai.*

Mash. see Bullock, C.

Nandi see Hollis, A.C. *The Nandi.*

Ovim. see Hambly, W.D.

Ton. see Junod, H.P. and Jaques, A.A.

Tonga see Milimo, J.T.

Tswana see Schapera, I.

Index of Biblical References

19.5	p.70
19.9	p.70
19.10	p.30.42
19.12	p.30
19.13	p.89
19.14	p.66.89.91.108
19.15	p.61
19.16	p.39
19.17	p.46.63.66
19.18	p.89
19.21	p.50.115
19.22	p.60
19.26	p.90.108
20.2	p.30
20.4	p.59.61
20.5	p.38
20.7	p.90
20.8	p.30.70
20.11	p.90
20.12	p.51.116 note 14
20.16	p.67
20.18	p.30.31
20.20	p.90.108
20.21	p.66.91
20.23	p.82 note 35
20.26	p.30
20.28	p.30
20.29	p.41.90.92.108
20.30	p.88
21.1	p.30
21.3	p.49
21.5	p.65
21.6	p.58
21.9	p.40.89.91.108
21.13	p.63
21.14	p.40
21.17	p.61
21.19	p.89.91.108
21.22	p.31